We're All
in this
Together

Praise for *We're All in this Together*

Abe Sass dove into poetry like he had been waiting all his life to put words on paper. It's been a heady ride watching him recapture his treasure trove of memories for friends old and new. In these poems Abe describes friends, foes, family, and passers-by with a keen eye for what connects us all. He believes in people, and his poetry reminds us of what matters in our lives. In his artist's statement, he mentions a few of these remarkable people: "A wounded soul in a mental health clinic, a kid from the block I grew up on, a kindred spirit at a rally for equal rights, a garment worker who tag-teamed with my mother, a mad man who danced on the street, an artist who turns steel into magic." These are just some of the characters you'll find in *We're All in this Together*. This is a book of big poems from a man with a big heart.

> *Bob Stanley*
> Sacramento Poet Laureate 2009-2012

Open the book to any page; inside *We're All in This Together,* poet and non-poet alike will be charmed by accessible poems expressed with the tender subversiveness of Abe Sass's imaginative words. Abe's poetry, in a kind of plain spoken grandeur, is witness to his sense of justice, deep feelings, and gift for storytelling. The ear as well as the spirit will delight in the ring of Abe's stanzas.

> *Connie Gutowsky*
> Author of *Play*

As a poet, Abe Sass possesses a special gift. It's his ability to engage the reader's heart and mind. His imagery is real. Not one ounce of pretension. His themes touch us all. You might find yourself reading his pieces out loud, only to discover that this is what they are really designed for.

> *Maria Nemeth*
> Author of *The Energy of Money*
> and *Rita Saenz*

We're All in this Together

poems by Abe J. Sass

For Janice —
For all these years, near and far —
You've been part of who we are —
Our lives are brighter, more
thoughtful, and you've been
a wonderful stimulus.
Thank you so much
All our love to you —
Abe

Cover Design by Lawrence Fox and Gerald Ward

ISBN: 978-1-941125-42-7

Library of Congress Control Number: 2015945213

Printed by I Street Press
at the Sacramento Public Library
828 I Street
Sacramento, California 95814
(916) 264-2777

First published 2015
Manufactured in the United States

DEDICATION AND THANK YOU

I am dedicating this book of poems to the two amazing women you see here, my wife Rivkah and my daughter Ilana. Their love surrounds me and enhances all I do.

Rivkah and Ilana's magic allows me to say to you, dear reader, "Here in this book are many of the people of my life, from the "Once upon a time" people to the "Here and Now" people.

So turn the page, come on in, they're all waiting for you!

My heartfelt thanks to Bob Stanley and Connie Gutowsky for their guidance and friendship.

Bob, about five years ago, you opened my door to writing poetry. You're a wise teacher, and your feedback, strong but gentle, mindful of me being the "new kid on the block" has been a brightly colored roadmap to extraordinary places.

Connie, your sense of balance and your way of helping me work toward more clarity has been a wonderful gift. I hear you now saying, "What would happen if you moved this over to here?"

So Bob and Connie, this new part of my life has your stamp on it.

ACKNOWLEDGMENTS

Previously published in *Late Peaches* (SPC Press, 2012):
    "Summer on West 18th"

Previously published by *Poems-for-all, Scattered like seeds*:
    "Watermelon Men"

Previously published in *Morning Coffee Anthology* (I Street Press, 2013):
    "August 28th, 1963"
    "Organic Carrot Juice"
    "Jury Duty, 2013"
    "It's Parkinson's"

Previously published in *Six Sacramento Poets* (2012):
    "Saturday Afternoon Matinee"
    "The Sacramento Dancer"
    "Another Flight Over the Cuckoo's Nest"
    "A College Christmas"
    "Langston"
    "Concertina Wire"
    "Watermelon Men"

Poems dramatized by The Actors Theatre of Sacramento in the stage play *River City Anthology* (2013):
    "Sacramento Sonata"
    "At the Funeral Parlor"
    "Donatella"
    "The Sacramento Dancer"

ARTIST'S STATEMENT

I believe life is random. Doors appear when we least expect them and we
never know what's on the other side. My career in Clinical Social Work, my
involvement in Social Justice and Civil Rights, my upbringing in New York
City and the love I receive from my amazing family, all lead me to say,
"Open the door and step on through to the other side."

Since moving to Sacramento I've stepped through many doorways. This
book represents one of them. Poetry has touched me. I follow pathways
into areas that say, "Remember me?" Sounds, smells, scenes, and people
appear from different times in my life, from the streets I grew up on to the
streets of downtown Sacramento, where I now live.

A wounded soul in a mental health clinic, a kid from the block I grew up on
who became my teacher, a kindred spirit at a rally for equal rights, a
garment worker who tag-teamed with my mother, a mad man who danced
on the street, an artist who turns steel into magic. These are some of the
people in my poems. They have all leaned over, put their arms around me
and whispered in my ear, "Come on, write about me."

- Abe J. Sass

TABLE OF CONTENTS

West 18th Street

It's What I Do

This Ain't the Fabulous Forties

West 18th Street

Too Young For Playing On The Stoop

Sitting on a blanket, on my ground floor fire escape
My toys all around me
On a hot summer day in New York
Looking up

I watch everybody
Hanging over their window sills
Shaking out their sheets and towels
A parade of dancing underwear and twirling dresses
Being reeled out on the lines
To the tune of squeaking pulleys

A canvas of clothes line color
Criss crossing the smudgey brick walls

Now and then a slight breeze sneaks over
From the back lot next door
I welcome its touch
Turn my head to catch it

Much later as evening comes on
And the apartment heat rages
"Can I go on the fire escape again, ma?"
She helps me gather more toys
I climb out with my little soldiers, my tanks, and my planes
Ready to fight the war with my army

As the battle reaches a frenzy
With explosions everywhere
It all stops

Voices come crashing down
Down through the underwear and the dresses on the lines
Down through the towels and the big floppy sheets
Voices come crashing down

 "Hey, get in that goddam bath tub, tomorrow's church."

"You're not wearin' that to church."

"Last week you didn't go to church, you're goin' this week, god dammit."

"After church we'll be at the tavern
You kids play on the stoop."

I was still too young for playing on the stoop
And horrified by their church
And yet it all seemed so exciting
And I knew I'd get there
Maybe not the church part
But hanging out on the stoop, oh yes!

Just Another Business Man

"Shoe laces, pencils, razor blades."
"Shoe laces, pencils, razor blades."

My mother has me by the hand
We're near 23rd Street and 8th Avenue
He's on a board with little wheels
He has no legs
I can see a belt and the tops of his trousers
But whatever else he has, is covered up
With a little raggedy brown blanket

"Shoe laces, pencils, razor blades."

His stuff is all spread out
In front of him on the sidewalk
My mom reaches into her pocketbook
Bends down, gives him some coins
He takes them in his flat spread out hand

"Hello sonny."

His eyes catch me
I try to get away

"Here sonny, you can have a pencil."

His face is all streaked with sweat
His hand holding up the pencil
Is dirty and raw in spots
No getting away

"Uuuhhhh," I can't speak

"It's ok," he says, "here take it
Your momma bought it, didn't you lady?"

"Yes I did, and thank you Mister."

"See sonny, it's ok with your momma
Go ahead, take it
You don't have to be scared of me
I'm just another business man."

My mom looks down at me
"Go ahead, Abraham, take the pencil."
I look up
She nods
I reach down to him
He looks right up, into me, and smiles

"It's an Eberhard Faber #2
Good for Drawing!"

I take it
"Th, th, th, thank you," tip toes out of my mouth

As we walk away I glance back
He's looking right at me

"Shoe laces, pencils, razor blades."

Summer On West 18th

The brick tenements suck the heat into the tiny apartments
Tormenting us all
The sweltering air pushes us out
Out onto the street
The gutter's so hot it's sticky
Heat dances on the cars
Bounces off the hoods
You burn your hands if you dare to touch
You can't go back inside
Or you'll be sizzled meat

So the shady stoop is where we go
Kenny, Waldo, Umberto,
Oliver, his sister Cleo and me
Just sitting
Just sweating
Just waiting for something to happen
And finally, it does

Kenny leaps up, jumps off the stoop
"Here comes my pop!"
He runs to his father
Whispers some stuff
All we hear is "can we, huh, can we, huh?"
His father laughs, looks over at us
"Yeah, yeah, OK, I'll get it."
"Chrissakes, gimme a minute."

And before we can squawk, Kenny's father reappears
With the wrench, magic wrench
With the board, magic board
He goes to the grey hydrant
Till now just a thing for dogs to piss on
He twists the plug off with the magic wrench
A few drops plop to the sidewalk
We gather round him, breathless
He's got the magic wrench on the top of the hydrant
Turning
From deep down we hear a gurgle
Turning
The sound gets deeper, louder
It's coming

It's coming
Yes, YES, and now it roars out
Pouring into the gutter
We leap into it!
Screaming, jumping, laughing
Running in the gushing water
Running in wild crazy circles
Water, water
Cold, cold
Wild, wet
Wet, wet!

Kenny's father laughs loud and straddles the hydrant
Holds the magic board under the flow
"HERE WE GO!" he roars
He brings up the board
Up, up comes the full force of the glorious water
Then he brings it down
Then up, down, up, and way up

Across the street
The newly arrived kids squeal
As suddenly they're totally soaked

More kids come running
"The pumps on! Hey the pump's on!"
The message bounces off the buildings on the block
The ladies who hang out over their window sills
Laugh and run downstairs
Some clutching their wide eyed babies
They slip off their shoes
And shriek as they step into
The glistening, wonderful water

The men, strut over, light up, and pass their beers around
Soon everybody's here
Mr. O'Brien grabs his wife and pulls her under
Suddenly everybody's pulling everybody under
We're all screaming, jumping, laughing
Running in the gushing water
Running in wild crazy circles

Water, water
Cold, cold
Wild, wet!
Wet, wet!

Me and Kenny
White and wet
Oliver and his sister, Cleo
Black and wet
Waldo and Umberto
Brown and wet
And all the rainbow colors of the block
All wet, wet, wet!

The Subway Grate

You know that picture of Marilyn Monroe?
The one where the breeze makes her white dress fly up
Way up
She's standing on a New York City subway grate
You know the one I mean
Well, if you were a kid, and if you could get close, real close
And if instead of looking up at her and her flying dress
(which would be the natural thing to do)
You look down, way down
You'd see all kinds of loose change
Sitting on the ground, way below that subway grate

And years before Marilyn Monroe stepped on that grate
We were a bunch of raggedy kids
Huddled together
Looking down at all that loose change

Kenny has his special lock tied to a long, long piece of twine
Waldo sticks a big, gooey wad of gum
To the bottom of that lock
And Kenny slowly lowers it down through the grate
Towards all that loose change

"Hold it, dammit, don't let it sway!" pipes Midgey
"Will you shut up!" yells Kenny, clutching the twine
"Hey Midgey, lay off, he's right over a quarter." I shout
Waldo jumps in, "C'mon Kenny get that mother."
"Here comes the train!"
Down goes the lock
"Got it!"
"Don't move it, let it stick, let it stick!"

The subway rumbles under the ground
The breeze rushes up
Dust and dirt flying
We all shut our eyes
Kenny holds the twine tight and steady
The gooey lock sits on the quarter
We wait till the train goes by

When the rumbling stops
Kenny slowly, slowly starts to pull up the lock
The quarter's edge showing

No yelling now
Just all of us holding our breath
Eyes bugging out

The lock starts to sway
"Steady, steady, keep it steady."
The lock rises to the bottom of the grate
Kenny slides his fingers through
We can't move
Slowly, slowly, Kenny pulls the lock through the grate
Twists off the quarter
Holds it up, way up
"Way to go!"
"Got that mother!"

Midgey yells from the next grate
"Hey you guys, look down here
We got a goddamn fortune down here!"

So, before Marilyn Monroe was there
Turning that grate into an icon
We were there
Getting that spot ready for her photo shoot
And now the photo shoot is over
She's over too
Whenever I see that picture
I think of the tender talent she had
And I see us raggedy kids
Huddled together on that grate
Fishing for loose change

Money On The Bed

Cousin Rose was always collecting money
Money for trees in Israel
Money for families on relief
Money for people out on strike
She always had a cause

Roberta, her daughter and me
We'd be under the bed hiding from the bad guys
Or out in her yard with our six shooters blazing
Or sitting on the floor deciding which doll of hers
Would be mother, father, sister or brother

Cousin Rose never said
Don't do this
Or don't do that
Don't go here
Or don't go there

The money Cousin Rose collected was on plates
Sitting on the bed
In her bedroom
Sometimes we played in there

I couldn't stop looking at all that money
There was so much of it
I knew Cousin Rose would never miss some of it
I didn't say a word to Roberta
But I knew how bad I wanted it

When Roberta went to help her mom
I couldn't stop my crazy racing mind
I couldn't stop my madly thumping heart
I couldn't stop my hands
I shoved the money in my pockets
And then I shoved some more
I shoved it deep

The next day was Saturday
Movie day at the Elgin Theatre
All us kids were there
Hunkered down in our seats
Giggling, making famous farting sounds

And me, treating everybody on the block
To sodas
To Raisinettes
To popcorn
To Good 'n Plenty
To Hershey bars

And up on the screen The Durango Kid
Blasted the bad guys
And rode off on his white stallion

And as he disappeared over the hill
I was planning how to get back
Into Cousin Rose's bedroom
Waiting for Roberta to go help her mom again

Still The Elgin Theatre

Me and Kenny were way down in our seats
Saturday at the Elgin Theatre
The most magic place for all our movie adventures
All you needed was a quarter
A quarter was hard to get

Today we were too nervous to watch the movie
We were waiting
Holding our breath
Waiting for the matron to head out to the lobby

"OK, now," Kenny whispered
I slipped out of my seat
Kept real low
Snuck to the exit door

Last Saturday Kenny pushed it open just a crack
No alarm, no squeak, no nothing
So we made a plan

Today, Martin, Waldo, Midgey
Oliver and Cleo were all waiting outside
Pitching pennies up against the side door of the Elgin
Being real cool
Just waiting

"Please, no alarm, please."
I pushed the door slowly
It opened a crack
No alarm

Five dark shapes slid in
Stayed real low
Scampered into seats
Settled in
Looked over at each other
Giggled

That giggle came up in my throat yesterday

The New York Times announced
The new season for The Joyce Theatre

14

New York's most magic place for dance adventures
The Martha Graham Dance Company
And a long list of dance programs
All coming to The Famous Joyce Theatre

But if you walk over to The Joyce Theatre
On 19th Street and 8th Avenue
And check out its fantastic Art Deco marquee
Built in 1941
And if you tell them you know
That back then it was The Elgin Theatre
Where all the kids from 18th street
Used to go on Saturdays
And you just want to take a peek
They just might let you in

If they do
Slowly head down the aisle
Scamper into a seat
Settle in
Look around
Giggle

See, it's still the Elgin Theatre
Home to all my magic movie adventures
And never in all those years
Did the matron ever catch me

The Saturday Afternoon Matinee

We're all on the stoop
Me, Kenny, Waldo. Martin and Midgey
Watching the old church across the street
Come down

They've been at it for a week
Big hunks of grey stone
Whomping down
Onto the sidewalk
Black dust swirling up
Red bricks
Crunching down
Onto the sidewalk
Brown smoke rings floating up

Guys with cruddy orange helmets
Running around
Piling it all up
Heavy trucks hauling
It all away

Jesus, Mary, and all the saints
Were the first to go
Then they hauled off
The stained glass windows
And the long wooden pews
The priests and the nuns
Had some kind of ceremony
And now it was all turning to junk

We're passing this big ceegar around
Midgey stole it from his father
Who was always too drunk to give a shit
We're all woozy, acting tough
Elementary school, ceegar smoking, big shots

Saturday afternoon on West 18th Street
We're taking in the free matinee
Across the street

After the trucks leave
The afternoon starts sliding away
We're still woozy on the stoop
I'm thinking, "No more ceegars for me."
But I said that last time
And I know I'd do whatever
Just to be hanging out
On the stoop

Suddenly Waldo jumps up
"Hey man, what is this?"
A long black hearse rolls up
To where the church was
We all watch as two guys in dark suits
Start wandering through what's left
Of the stones and the bricks
They're carrying big cloth sacks
Soon they're bending down
Picking stuff up
Putting stuff in the bags
All real slow like

"They're bones, Man."
"Bones?"
"Yeah, bones"
"Like people bones?"
"Sure looks like it."

This show is getting too creepy
But we don't move
We just stare

After a while the guys in suits
Get in the hearse
And roll away

We look at each other
We look across the street
We're all thinking the same thing
"Come on."
"Uuuhhh, I don't know."
"Don't be a chicken"

"I ain't no chicken."

"Come on then!"
We're off the stoop
We're in what's left of the old church
I see bones peeping out of the ground
We're all looking down
Our eyes all buggy wide
"Oh Jesus," Martin screams
"It's a skull!"
And there we are
All looking right at it
"Whoa, this is too weird."

Kenny says, "Wait."
And runs back across the street
Disappears into the house
In a few minutes he's back
With some paper bags, his eyes all bright and wide
"Let's Keep some!"

Just that fast
 We drop all the creepy feelings
Suddenly, Me, Midgey, Waldo, Martin, and Kenny
We're all looking for bones
We pick them up
We toss them in the bags
We're on a crazy mission
We even get one one more skull
And Midgey claims it
After a while we get five bags of bones
And two skulls

It's almost dark now
We all gotta go in
Kenny says, "Put them under our stairs
We'll figure out what to do tomorrow."
"Tomorrow's church," says Midgey
Kenny chuckles
"Hey, where you think we been all day!"

We laugh as we carry the bags across the street
And stuff them under the stairs
At 320 West 18th Street
Where Kenny, Waldo, and I live

We all look down at the bags
Then we're looking at each other
Martin shakes his head
"We don't say nothing to nobody, ok?"

As everybody heads home
I open the door to my apartment on the ground floor
As I walk in I turn around
I can see a brown paper bag
Sticking out from under the stairs
I close the door fast

My mother's got supper ready
"Wash your hands," she says
As I head to the bathroom, she calls out
 "Is the church all gone yet?"
"Yeah, just about."

Sunday Morning

On Sunday morning
I'd wait for the knock on my door

"Hey, we're back from church
If you wanna, come on up."
Kenny always said that
He knew, knew I was waiting
Waiting to climb the stairs
Up to his apartment

His mom opens the door, smiles
Kenny and his dad
On the floor
The comics all spread out
A carpet of colors and shapes
Scattered there for us to giggle at
Scattered there for us to hold our breaths at
And Kenny's dad, reading and laughing out loud

After a while we'd all be eating sandwiches
On the floor
"Hey, don't spill stuff on the comics!"

I didn't want it to end
But it always did
They'd go visit some relatives
And I'd go back downstairs

When I got a little older
Sometimes on Sunday I'd buy The Daily News
Spread the comics out on the floor
A carpet of colors and shapes
And wish for a Dad who'd read and laugh out loud

Come, You Should See This

They stopped banging on the heat pipes hours ago
The super shoveled all the coal he was gonna shovel that night
The yelling from the apartments above
Had finally ground down
My mother's graham crackers and milk
Had put me to sleep

Her hand on my shoulder
Shakes me awake
"Ma, whaddaya doin'?"
The fuzz in my eyes tells me
It's not even morning
"Ma, lemme sleep."
"Come, you should see this."
"What?"
"Come, outside on the street."
"Ma!"
"I'll wait in the kitchen
Get dressed, come."
"Ok, ok..."

Soon I'm in the hallway, following her
Sleep still fogging my brain
She pushes the front door open
The cold jump starts my body
Snaps my eyes open
"Now look!"
I look
Out onto 18th Street

My street of rusty brown and grey tenements
My street of cracked sidewalks, dirty stoops and dented garbage cans
The street we play our city games on
Johnny Ride The Pony
Stoop Ball
Marbles in the gutter

The street is gone, all gone
A bright, cleansing light has come
Wrapping it up in soft whiteness
Snow drifting down, covering 18th Street
Covering my whole world

I hear the hush of no city sounds
"Look, look!" my mother points
Her hand makes a sweeping motion
Towards the street

I see silent creatures beckoning

The street lights
Now hooded
Wink down on me
Little white mounds of fillagree round their heads

The fire escapes
Now starkly highlighted
The shapes and swirls of their designs all moving
Playing their game of white and black, black and white

The standing, silent cars
All covered, all thick, all heavy
Giant animals resting
Slowly growing, changing shape

The street, the gutter, the sidewalk
A canvas, so smooth, pure white
No foot prints, no tire tracks
No dirt, no trash
Clean, clean

Her hand on my shoulder
Shakes me
I look up
She smiles
"Enjoy it all now
By the time you go to school in the morning
It will all be slush."

May Day

Mom took me by the arm
"Today we march," she said
May Day
She was ILGWU
She was union
She was quiet and brave

Esther, Tom and Marian
Miriam and Minerva
All our friends were there
I was just a kid
I was glad
I was scared

Everyone who was not marching
Down 8th Avenue
Was standing, screaming at us
Throwing stuff at us
We ducked the tomatoes
We ducked the eggs
We ducked the shaking fists
"Commies, go back to Russia!"
With Tom on one side
Mom on the other
Esther in front of me
I felt safe

"You want to hold the sign?" Tom asked
Oh, did I!
"Local 22, ILGWU."
I was just a kid
I will always be that kid
Proud, scared, holding my sign
Going down the avenue into tomorrow

At Esther's Table

At Esther's table they were all passionate
Proud to be Union
Proud of their solidarity
Proud of their work for justice
Men and women and us kids

The kitchen was small
But everyone fit around that well worn table at
350 West 18th Street, New York City
Sometimes Esther would stop at the car
Parked across the street
"Why don't you FBI guys go catch a crook." She'd say
They never smiled, just sat there
Watching
Protecting the country from Esther
And her "Un-American Activity" family and friends

But on Friday night, when the week's work was done
Everyone gathered
Time to spread butter on thick slices of Rye bread
Time to drink Tom and Esther's wine and dip into their goulash
Time to hear the stories, sing the songs
Time for laughing and slapping the table
 We were all making a better world

Now and then Esther would go downstairs
And offer a glass of home made wine
To the FBI guys
Esther's daughter Marian and I
Kids with wide eyes
Just watching
Wishing we were grown ups

We're From The FBI

The summer of 1953 was over
J. Edgar Hoover, Joe McCarthy and their cronies
Were bulldozing the country
It was a time of fear and horror

As Esther walked back to her apartment house
She carried her bags of groceries
She saw them both as they stepped from their car
Esther held her bags tighter
They approached
She felt her stomach quiver

They stood directly in her path
Forcing her to stop
"We're from the FBI
We're here to talk to you."

Whenever Esther would least expect them
They'd show up
Sometimes they'd just sit in their car
And watch
Who goes in
Who goes out
Sometimes Esther would bring out a glass of wine
"Here, try some wine
Then why not go and catch a crook."
They never even blinked

Occasionally they'd get out of their car
Cross the street
Always the same greeting
'We're from the FBI
We're here to talk to you."

But today was different
VERY, VERY different

Esther had not seen them
Since before that summer of 1953

Esther, constantly investigated
Constantly harassed

"We know you're a communist."
"We know you were at those meetings."
"Come on now, who else was there?"
"What were their names?"

Long before that Summer of 1953
Esther's daughter Marian and I grew up together
She was the sister I never had
We went from playing with toys
To marching for people's rights
To singing at rallies
With people like
Paul Robeson and Pete Seeger
Marian's favorite book was Madame Curie
And just before that summer of 1953
She was accepted to the Bronx High School of Science
Her dream school

Then she went away to summer camp
She never came back
Polio was loose on the land
Polio caught her
Followed her to the hospital
Killed her there
In that summer of 1953

And now they stood there
Directly in Esther's path
Forcing her to stop
"We're from the FBI
We're here to talk to you."

BUT today was different
VERY, VERY different

As her grocery bags exploded
Onto the street
A wild, untamed sound
Locked deep within Esther's soul broke loose
It roared out
Hot fury exploding
It crashed into all the buidings

Walls tumbled down

Windows shattered
The sidewalk cracked open

But all the people were safe and unafraid
And as we all gathered around Esther
Holding her
Loving her
A car with two men drove away
And never came back

They Gotta Come First

A woman was next to me
Looking up at me
As I stood at the Safeway Deli Counter

"Excuse me, would you
Please buy a small piece of chicken
For me?"
"Small" was the word she used
Not this piece
Not that piece
Not dark meat
Not light meat
Just small
"A small piece of chicken."

The man behind the counter
Quickly leaned over
"Oh ma'am we don't allow that in the store."
She stammered as her words fell to the floor
"I'm so sorry,
I didn't mean any harm
I apologize."

In that stab of a moment
I'm a kid again, back on West 18th Street, in New York City
And there's Mike, coming down the block
Clip clop, clip clop
Mike, the Ice Man
And his horse, Mabel, pulling the wagon
Clip clop, clip clop
He pulls on the reins
"Whoa Mabel."

His wagon, faded blue, turning grey, comes to a stop
Mike jumps down from the high front seat
He gently hooks the brown bag of oats
Round Mabel's head
Little red ribbons hang from the cord
Mike pats Mabel's long grey nose
Then climbs into the back of the wagon

Mabel settles in and as us kids reach up to pet her
We inhale the sweet aroma of the oats
A soft murmur shimmies up from her throat

Mike pulls out some burlap sacks
And starts to chip away at the big blocks of ice
We run to the back of the wagon and watch
"Here you go!" he laughs
And throws his treasures to us

We catch the shiney pieces
And the sweet cold taste of ice chips
Tickles my mouth

"Mike, some more, Mike!"
He laughs again
"Oh yeah, but first you kids gotta work!"

He chips some more and the ice cracks wide open
Big hunks slide around the floor of the wagon
He puts the ice hunks in the burlap sacks
And hands them down to us
Kenny, Martin, Waldo, Oliver and me
We each grab a sack
We stand there, looking up

We know what Mike's gonna say
Mike says it every time
And we know it by heart

"Those hunks are for the people
Who don't have enough money
They gotta come first."

We each head out on our mission
I carry my ice hunk to Mrs. Sullivan's apartment
She's real sick and she's on relief
"Thank you Abraham
You're a good boy, even if you're a Jew."

I see Kenny climbing the stairs to old Mr. Shaunessy's place
His burlap sack turning dark
As the water drops
Drip on through
We're running all over the block
Leaving little drops behind
For the sun to swallow up

When we all return our backs are wet
But the cold feels good
Mike smiles and throws us some more ice chips
We suck them in
I rub some in my hair
Let the water drip down my face

We all know what's next

"OK, now for the others."
He fills our sacks again
And back we go
Running, climbing stairs
Stuffing the money we get into our pockets
To give to Mike

When we're all done
Mike gives us a few coins
"Good job."
As we stand next to Mabel
Petting her
A soft murmur shimmies up from her throat

Mike climbs back up, into the wagon
"OK, now off you go
See you kids next time."

As we all walk over to the stoop
Mike waves to us and softly chants
"Ok Mabel, gee yap."

As Mike and Mabel slowly start off
He looks right down at me
Right into my head

"Abraham, you go tell that guy behind that Safeway counter
You gotta take care of the people
Who don't have enough money
They gotta come first."

As Mike and Mabel
Slip back into my memory
I turn to the woman standing beside me
I look down at her
"C'mon, let's me and you go get some chicken."

The Last Ice Wagon

We were playing stoop ball
When we heard the siren
Me, Waldo, Kenny and Oliver
Looked over, toward 8th Avenue
Sure to see a fire engine or an ambulance go by

But the siren sound
Wound down
Slow like
And stopped

When you live on West 18th Street
A siren is just another city noise
But this one stopped
Right on the corner

Then we heard more sirens
Screaming
Winding down
Slow like
Stopping
Right on the corner

We knew something real bad happened

As we started towards 8th Avenue
The sound of another siren
Bounced down 18th Street

We were running now
Turning the corner
Pushing through people

A man blocked our way
"You kids don't need to see this
Go on back home."
He tried to hold us back
Then gave up
As we shoved ahead
Towards the front of the crowd

Mike's crushed Ice Wagon
Was on its side
His horse, Mabel
Was sprawled in the gutter
Shaking, snorting
Trying to get up
Falling back down
Blood everywhere

Mike was on the ground
His arms around Mabel's head
Screaming, crying out
"NO, NO, NO, NO
PLEASE GOD
OH GOD
NO, NO, NOOO!"
A cop tried to pull Mike off Mabel
But couldn't

The car that hit her
Was on the sidewalk
A guy, sitting in the street
Was holding his head, crying

As the cops pushed us all back
I saw a huge, grey New York City utility truck pull up
The cops were everywhere
They blocked our view

Then we all heard a sharp crack
And another

Me, Kenny, Waldo and Oliver
Stood there
Lost

Then we saw the back of the huge truck
Tip up
They hooked a chain to Mabel
And slowly pulled her up
Into the truck

Mike stood there, crying

Some of the people from the block
Were next to Mike, their arms around him
Kenny said, "C'mon let's go over."
We followed him over to Mike
Mike put his hand down
Patted our heads

We never saw Mike again

The other day
In Sacramento
I heard a familiar clip clopping sound
I turned to see
A big wagon
Pulled slowly by a team of two horses
As they passed me
The driver shook the reins
And yelled out
"Gee yap."

And the sweet, cold taste of ice chips
Once again, tickled my mouth

Father Maloney

"Don't get too close to Father Maloney
Or he'll grab your ass."
Midgey went for Kenny's ass
Kenny jumped out of the way
"Hey Midgey, you're not funny, you're just stupid!"
Waldo joined in
"Midgey, you in one of your dumb moods again?"

Me, Kenny, Waldo and Midgey
Were hanging out on the stoop
Just messing around
After a while it all got boring
So we were heading up 18th Street
To get some "loosies"
2 cigarettes for a nickel
At the candy store on the corner

Old man Delgado kept them in a cup
Under the counter
He'd bring it out when us neighborhood kids came in

As we neared the corner
Waldo stopped, turned to Midgey
"You're one of Father Maloney's alter boys, right?"
"Yeah."
"He really do that?"
"Do what?"
"Grab your ass?"
Midgey looked down
"Yeah....sometimes."
"Jeez, I'm glad I don't go to St. Bernard's."

I watched
Not wanting to know what the hell they were talking about
Just glad I wasn't a Catholic

Old man Delgado smiled as we came in
Reached down, pulled up the cup
"It's gonna be hot today
You kids want a soda too? My treat."

A few weeks later, me, Kenny, and Waldo were on the stoop
"Hey Abraham, you hear about Father Maloney?" asked Kenny
"No, why would I hear about Father Maloney?"
"Very funny."
"They moved him to St. Bartholomews, over on the east side
Waldo looked over, "Bet Midgey's happy."

Later Midgey showed up
No body mentioned Father Maloney

After a while we got bored and Kenny said
"Let's head up to Delgado's
And get some loosies
Maybe he'll throw in a soda."

New Kid On The Block

Me, Kenny and Waldo
Sitting on the stoop
Laughing
Just getting home from Saturday's movie
Still seeing Abbot and Costello
Run like hell
From Frankenstein, Wolf Man
And all the other usual suspects

We see him
Coming up the block
The new kid

He walks slow
Comes to the stoop
Looks at us
"Can I come up?"

Kenny looks at him
Looks at us
Shrugs
"Yeah, free country."

"Hey, you from Puerto Rico?" Asks Waldo
"Yeah."
"Me too."
"Tu nombre?"
"Claudio."

I never saw Waldo
Do an introduction before
He points to us and grins
"That's Kenny
He's Abraham
Me, I'm Waldo."
Just like grown ups do

"How long you been here?" asks Waldo
"Just got here."
Me and Kenny watch
As the two of them jump into life in Puerto Rico

"Hey, do you know...?"
"Oh man, I been there and do you...?"
"My grandma and everybody
They never gonna leave..."
"Yeah I sure do miss it."
"You really gonna miss it
When winter comes."
Me and Kenny laugh and hang on for the ride
As Waldo and Claudio go on and on

After a while
I spot Midgey
Coming up the block

Claudio sees him too
Gets up right away
"See you, I gotta get home
We're having birthday cake
For my little sister
She's 5."

Waldo yells out
"Hey, me and Abraham here, we like chocolate
Kenny, he eats anything."
Claudio smiles
Then turns and heads down the block

When Midgey gets to the stoop
He sits down
Stares at us
"How you guys know that kid?"

"We just met him," I say
"Yeah, he's from Puerto Rico too
Same neighborhood as me," laughs Waldo

"Well, I got news for you guys," snarls Midgey
That kid you just met
I don't give a shit where he's from
He's a goddamn faggot."

Me, Kenny and Waldo
Just look at each other

Waldo slowly gets up
Looks down at me and Kenny
"I gotta go in now
You guys wanna come?'
"Yeah," I say, getting up
"Yeah," I'm comin' too," says Kenny
"Hey, I'll come too." says Midgey

Waldo turns, looks down at him
"Some other time, Midgey
But in the meantime
Why don't you just go fuck yourself."

Forbidden Fruit

A can of Vienna sausage
Winked at me the other day
As I was walking down the aisle
At the Sacramento Safeway
I winked back
I smiled
Started to reach out
Suddenly
I heard my mother's voice
"FEH, never in my house!"

Me, Kenny and Waldo played hookey
It was a thing we did

When Waldo would announce
"Hey, nobody's gonna be home tomorrow
Whaddya say?"
We didn't have to say much
We just knew

"Ma, I feel terrible, real bad
 I think I may even have a fever."
"Well, Abraham, maybe you need to stay home today."
"Yeah, maybe you're right."
Then my mom would head out the door
To her job in that sweat shop

Kenny was really good
At throwing up
He'd run to the bathroom
Slam the door
And you'd think he was gonna die
But he had to convince his mother AND his father
Then they would head out the door
To their jobs at the box factory

I'd cross the hall
Kenny would come downstairs
And we'd meet at Waldo's apartment
We'd count our change
Plan our next move

Lots of times we'd wander up to 42nd Street
Get a slice of pizza or a frank
Then go shop lifting in the stores

Later we'd huddle in a doorway
Chuckling as we swapped stories
Of our little crime wave
As we examined each other's loot

Some grown up would always yell
"Shouldn't you kids be in school?"
Kenny would yell back
"Aaah. go peddle your papers."

Later we'd wind up back at Waldo's
Waldo would grin
Then he'd open the cupboard
There they sat
A bunch of them
Little blue cans
Vienna Sausage

My mother NEVER had Vienna sausage
I'd maneuver her down the grocery aisle
And plead
"C'mon ma, just one can."
She'd scrunch up her face
"FEH, never in my house!"

Waldo's folks loved them
Had lots of them
We'd dip our fingers into the thick grease
Pull them out
Eat them slowly
One by one
Then lick the delicious grease off our fingers

We'd belch and fart
For the rest of the afternoon
Then Waldo would check the clock
"We'd better clean this shit up
Or my pop's gonna kick my ass."

We'd hurry
Pick up everything
Then carry it down
To the garbage cans in the basement
Bury it deep

A can of Vienna sausage
Winked at me the other day
As I was walking down the aisle
At the Sacramento Safeway

I winked back
I smiled
Started to reach out
Suddenly
I heard my mother's voice
"FEH, never in my house!"

The Captain Of The Ship

When the kids would ask
I'd say, "My father died."
Today we're sitting on the stoop
And Midgey says, "Hey Abraham, how'd he die?"

Waldo puts down his comic book
Kenny stops dinking around with his two little
Black and white dog magnets
Oliver stops bouncing his spauldeen
Martin stares over at me
"Hey Abraham, you don't have to answer him
That's your business
Midgey's just trying to fuck with you."

"Yeah, I know."

"Hey Martin, you don't need to protect him," says Midgey

I look right at Midgey
"OK, I'll tell you once, but I'm not gonna tell you again. OK?"

"OK."

The words come out of me
Like they do when I'm sitting on the stoop
On Sunday nights
Telling spooky stories
To the kids from 18th Street
And I start feeling like
The Home Run King

My father's the Captain Of The Ship
He's patrolling enemy waters
Out of the night the torpedo strikes hard
The explosion lights up the sky
The ship splits open
My father does not leave the men
Trapped below the decks
And the ship sinks beneath the waves

As I finish my story, nobody says a word
Except Midgey
"Hey Abraham, I swear man, I didn't know."

Later, when we all get up
And head back to our apartments
I push the hallway door open
And walk to apartment number 3
Where me and my mother live

And I feel like
The Home Run King

At the Funeral Parlor

He was some old guy who died
I didn't know him
Neither did most of us kids on the block
He was Catholic
And a regular at the tavern
And everybody's folks knew him

We were all on the stoop, spotting cars
"49 Chevy.
"48 Ford."
Suddenly Martin jumps up
"Shit, we gotta go to the funeral parlor."
"Ugh, man, I don't wanna go."
"We gotta go."
"Abraham, you gotta go too."
"Yeah, it don't matter if you're not Catholic."
"You ever see a dead body?"
"No, you?"
"No."

So we all went
The place was kinda dark
Candles, burning all over
One of those big crosses over the coffin
We slowly walked to the front
This guy with shiny hair and dark suit made us line up
The grown ups had already gone up

One by one us kids approached
Kneeled on the little padded stool
In front of the coffin
Made the sign of the cross and moved to the side

I watched, scared
My turn was coming
I memorized every move
What if I don't do it right?
Could I drop dead?
Get some curse?

Kenny, my best friend, was next
So smooth
Bowed his head, kneeled
Touched his forehead
His chest
Then one shoulder
Then the other
Moved to the wall

I don't remember what I did
But I did something
And it must have been OK
Because later as we went back outside
Midgey, my arch enemy said
"Not bad for a kike."
Kenny jumped in as he always did
"Come on, cut it out.
Let's go get a soda."

We all got our sodas
And sat on the stoop
"47 Plymouth."
"Whoa, check it out , 49 Caddy!"

Midgey

Midgey came round the corner on his bike
My mood was dark as I sat on the stoop
Midgey had been on my case for days
Kept seeking me out whenever he could
I was tired of hiding out in my apartment

"Hey Jew boy! Jew boy!"
He hit his brake and laughed
Most days it was, "Oh fuck you" as I'd turn and head inside
But today wasn't one of those days

I don't remember anything
But I know I jumped off the stoop
Straight at Midgey

I hear screaming in my head
I'm tumbling on the ground
With me on Midgey
I'm tumbling on the ground
With Midgey on me
I hear shrieks
From me?
From him?

There's no me
There's no him
It's us all locked together

"Hey you kids, break it up!"
"C'mon, break it up!"
Hands pulling us apart

Suddenly I see him
Blood all over his mouth, his nose
His eye is twitching

"Break it up, goddammit."

Somebody's holding him
Somebody's holding me

"Hey Midgey, you better get on home
And check out your nose!"

All I want to do is sit down and hold my head
Mr. O'Brien from upstairs is next to me
He sits down, puts his arm around me
"Jesus, you guys were killing each other."

Suddenly I'm crying
"Hey, it's ok, it's ok."
I just can't stop
Mr. O'Brien keeps his arm around me
"It's ok, it's ok, you sure gave it to Midgey."
I look up at him
"Yeah," he smiles
I feel myself smiling too

After a while my shuddering and my crying stop
Mr. O'Brien is still on the stoop
With his arm round my shoulder

A few days later
I'm on the stoop with Kenny, Martin and Waldo
Midgey and his Uncle walk over
He has a big bandage on his nose

His Uncle leans down and whispers to him
Midgey shakes his head
His Uncle whispers again
Midgey looks up at him
"Do I gotta?"
I hear his Uncle say, "Yeah."
Midgey looks up at me
"Hey, sorry."
I shake my head
"OK."
Midgey slides over onto the stoop
His Uncle walks away
Everybody's back
Sitting on the stoop

Basic Training

Me and Waldo
Were walking up 8th avenue
Heading to 23rd street
To catch a movie at the RKO

"Hey Abraham."
Can I tell you something?"
"Uh huh."
"Man, you gotta walk tough."
"Whaddya mean?"
"I mean tough
You don't look tough
I know you're a Jew
But you can still walk tough."

Waldo, one of my best friends
But I never looked at how he walked
I never even looked at how I walked

"Look, Abraham
These Irish kids
Always want to fuck with you
They used to fuck with me too
They all hate spics and kikes
But they don't fuck with me, anymore."
Wanna know how come?"

As we crossed the street
I turned to him
"Yeah, I sure do."

"My big brother, Rodrigo
Showed me how to walk tough
I know you ain't got no big brother
And you ain't got no father, right?"
I shook my head
"Yeah."

"Well, you want me
To show you how?"
"Yeah."

That day was the
Start of basic training

On the way home from the RKO
Waldo turned to me
"OK? Ready?"

I took a deep breath
"Yeah, ready."

"OK, watch me
You gotta be smooth
But you gotta be tight
Keep your ass tight
You gotta swing your arms
You gotta take long steps
See? Watch me."

I was watching
I stayed with him
Swinging my arms
Taking long steps
Keepin' my ass tight

"Now, you gotta squint your eyes
That makes you look real tough."

Soon I was
Walking smooth
Walking tight
Ass tight
Arms swinging
Long steps
Eyes squinting

Waldo turned to me
"You got it."

We walked that way
All the way home, to 320 West 18th street
Waldo lived in apartment #5
I lived in apartment #3

As we walked into the hallway
We smiled at each other
"See ya tomorrow."
"Yeah, see ya, thanks."

Now and then
I still catch myself

Walking smooth
Walking tight
Taking long steps
Ass tight
Arms swinging
Eyes squinty
I smile and think of Waldo

The Hudson River Pier

Long before Pete Seeger
Stood on the deck of the Sloop Clearwater
Long before his crew
Started cleaning up the Hudson
We were walking up West 18th Street
On a hot Saturday afternoon
Heading to the river

We didn't think about mucky water
All we thought about was
"It's hot, let's go to the river
And jump off the pier."

Me and Waldo were the best swimmers on our block
Waldo moved here from Puerto Rico
Where he swam a lot
Me, I had gone away to summer camps
Since I was about seven
Anything to do with water
Was just right for me

Kenny and Oliver
Were good at jumping in
They'd swim some
Then head back to the pier

Sometimes Midgey would join us
He'd slide in and mostly hold on
Now and then he'd push off a little
Splash around and get back real fast

Today me and Waldo were swimming near the pier
Midgey was in the water
Holding onto the pier
Oliver and Kenny had been in already
They were sitting on the pier
Dripping wet

Waldo yelled over to Midgey
"Vente, Midgey, seas hombre!"
I chimed in
"Yeah, c'mon, don't be a chicken."

Oliver yelled down from the pier
"C'mon Midgey, don't be scared
A little water won't kill you."

Midgey called me kike and Christ killer tons of times
But I'd never heard what came out of his mouth now
"Fuck you, nigger."
Oliver's eyes opened wide
He leaped up
Ran to the edge of the pier

At that very moment Midgey did it
He did it big
He pushed off
Off into the river

His hands were going up and down
He was kicking his feet wildly
Making gigantic splashes
His head was twisting side to side
He was coming further out
Towards me and Waldo
Twisting, splashing, kicking
He kept it up
Then it happened

Midgey went under
Then his head came back up
Then he went down again
This time when he came back up
His arms were flailing around
His eyes were wide open
Water was pouring from his mouth
He went under again
Splashing wildly
As he came up again
He screamed, "Help me!"

Me and Waldo started for him
Swimming as hard as we could
We reached him

Grabbed him
Tried to hold him up
Get him back to the pier

Oliver and Kenny jumped in
Somehow we all pulled him to the pier
Held him up
Struggled to catch our breath

As we all climbed onto the pier
Midgey couldn't stop crying

We all sat there for a long time
Nobody said anything
Midgey kept gasping and coughing
"You wanna go to the hospital?" asked Kenny
"No."

When the gasping and the coughing stopped
Midgey looked over at all of us
He didn't say anything
Oliver looked at Midgey, shook his head
Got up and said, "Whadda you say we all go home."

We got up and slipped our clothes
Over our wet underpants
As we started back
Midgey said he was going
To his Uncle's place on 17th Street
He crossed the street and disappeared

Oliver turned to us
"Hey what is with him?"
Kenny laughed
"Hey you guys
I'm the only one he's got no bad names for."
Waldo chuckled
"Yeah, you're right, it pays to be Irish.
Abraham's the kike, I'm the spic, now you're the nigger."
Oliver shook his head
"We should start a club."

Welcome Home

Hey Francis
When I grew up on West 18th Street
I never saw you walking down the block
Looking for a fight

When Midgey and his little cousin
Announced to me, after their catechism class
"Hey Jew boy, you goddam Christ killer."
I know you were somewhere else

When Claudio got beat up on 17th street
After coming out of Delgado's candy store
I never heard you yell
"Hey faggot, don't come round here no more."

When Oliver was walking down the block
From an open window
On the 3rd floor
Somebody yelled, "go home, nigger'"
If you'd been there
I know you would have proudly walked
Right alongside Oliver

Now, all these years later
You show up
Well, they say, "better late than never."

And Francis
Now that you run the show
And they call you Pope
I know a lot of people
Are really pissed off at you

And wherever you were then
You're sure on the street now
Scaring the devil
Out of all the bigots and racists
And all the homophobes
Especially when you said, "Who am I to judge?"

But I know you can handle the devil
Hell, he's just small potatoes on your plate

So keep doing what you're doing
And don't let it get to you

'Cause the rest of us are glad you showed up
Welcome home and we've got your back

Waiting For Mr. Muniz

Mr. Muniz worked nights at the bakery
Saturday mornings we'd smell him
Coming home
Up five flights of stairs

We'd lean over the banister
Breathing him in
Rubbing our bellies
Wildly waiting
Me and Robert Muniz
5th grade buddies

What'll he bring home today?
Cinnamon rolls?
Eclairs?
Donuts?"
Raisin bread?

As he turns to us on the 5th floor landing
He is all delicious aroma
A fine cloud of white flour
Sharp against his black hair
The flecks of delicious wonder
That cling to his shirt
Announce his entrance

His dark gentle eyes touch Robert
Touch me
"Ah Roberto, mi hijo.
Ah Abram, Buenos dias."
"Hi Mr. Muniz."
"Poppa, whatchyougot?"
"Ha ha, you'll see!"

The door to apartment 5B is wide open
Mrs. Muniz has set the little kitchen table
With the magic of
Hot chocolate
Hot coffee
Fresh squeezed orange juice

And as Robert and I follow Mr. Muniz
Into the apartment
The dancing air
Rich with sweetness
Follows us!

Freeman

Part One

The old super up and left
One cold winter day
Just disappeared
Left his booze bottles behind
And an old dog eared dog
Mrs. Kelley took it to the ASPCA
And now we got a new super

My mother said, "He's a nice Negro man,
He doesn't curse, doesn't get drunk
Like Mr. Sullivan."
"Yeah," I said, rushing out the door, heading to high school

I'd never been down in the basement
Where the supers lived
They all seemed so grumpy and mean
The new super was different
Smiled, said hello
Always busy
Hauling the garbage cans out
Mopping under the stairs
Where the old drunks peed
I grew up in that building
First time that hallway didn't stink

One time I saw the new super carrying Mrs. Gunderson's groceries
Up the stairs
Mrs. Gunderson, with her bent up back
Steadying herself with that crooked cane
"Now you be careful ma'am"
She lived on the top floor
Five flights of stairs

Sometimes, on the way to school
I'd see the coal truck come
Dump Its load down the chute into the cellar
Black dust swirling in the cold air
The driver steadying the chute, coughing
The super shoveling it into a big pile

BANG, BANG, BANG
They'd rap on the steam heat pipes
All the people above us
Banging for more heat
We lived on the ground floor
Apartment #3
Never worried about heat
Sometimes they'd yell down the air shaft
"Hey, get some heat up here, goddamn it."
Sometimes they'd spice it up with "damn nigger."

One night the water pipe under our sink broke
Water oozing out all over the floor
I ran down to the super
He opened the door
As soon as I told him, he grabs a satchel with tools
"Don't worry, we"ll fix it."
As he was shutting the door I peered inside
A little table with an open book on it
A saggy brown couch and a metal stand up lamp
Throwing a soft light
A guitar leaning against the wall
Some pictures on the wall

I follow him up
Soon he's on the floor
Head under the sink
Pulling and yanking and grunting
And the water stops
"Thank you so much," my mother says
As she holds the mop
The super looks right at me
Shiney light in his eyes
"Now you grab that mop from your mother
And get on it while I run down and get another mop."
And he did
And we mopped
And I felt real good

Later my mother says
"Would you like some tea?"
His eyes do that shiney look again
"Well, the water's in the pipe where it's supposed to be
And we done got it up off the floor
And tea would be fine."
"What's your name?" asked my mother
"Freeman."
"Freeman, that's a beautiful name, " she says
"Thank you, ma'am"
"I'm Sylvia, and you know my son, Abraham"
"Yes, ma'am, he's a good mopper!"

Part Two

It was summertime
The windows were open
The air was wet and hot
From down in the basement I heard
A harmonica wailing
A guitar twanging
And cutting in and out of it
Freeman singing loud and strong
The blues coming up through the floor
Sliding through the slats of the fire escape
Bouncing off the airshaft walls

Soon I'm knocking at his door
Soon I'm sitting on his couch
Soon we're laughing
"You got a Jew's harp?"
Freeman laughs, slaps his leg
"Now Abraham, you go on upstairs
And get that Jew's harp
Let's make some music."

> *Goin' to Kansas City*
> *Kansas City here I come*
> *They got a lotta crazy women there*
> *And man, I'm gonna get me one*

Freeman's stompin' his feet
Slappin' his guitar
His harmonica is screamin'
He's singin' loud and strong
And me, I'm hittin' on my Jew's harp

Later on
I'm still sitting on his couch
The harmonica and the Jew's harp
Are on the table
The guitar's leaning against the wall
Freeman and I have crossed the border
And he takes me on a journey

"Abraham, I had to go real bad
The colored bathroom was locked
I tried but I couldn't hold it no longer
And I soiled myself real bad."
No shiney look now
Just tears swelling up in his eyes
And all I can do is shake my head

"Abraham, you know this ain't no honey of a job
But, you know, I'm never goin' back to Mississippi
I'm a free man now."
I smiled
"Free Man. Freeman."
"Yeah, Free Man, my mother had a lot of names
On her mind
Freeman was the one she picked. Free Man."

Brandy

One day Freeman, my super, said
"Abraham, you wanna take Brandy for walks?"
That day a whole chunk of my life changed

Brandy was his golden Great Dane
A new arrival from a friend of his
Who moved away

"Abraham, those Catholic kids
Won't fuck with you
When you're with Brandy."

That night Freeman showed me how to walk with her
How to hold her leash
How to say, "Guard."
For a few days I hung out in Freeman's apartment
Playing with Brandy
She felt like my dog
Freeman chuckled, "You the man, now."
Then Brandy and I started walking

I didn't just walk with her
I bounced
The first time the 17th street kids approached me
On 8th avenue
I held her leash and looked straight ahead
They got a little too close
I said "Guard."
Brandy looked at them and growled
They never got close again

The best part of Freshman High School year
Was the new me
And my new buddy, Brandy

It's What I Do

It's What I Do

Words always played mean tricks on me
They'd whisper in my ear
"Maybe we will come out."
"Maybe we will not come out."
"You'll never know when."
A cruel game
It followed me everywhere

"Here c, c, c, c, comes Abraham."
I'd hear it
 As I walked down the block
The kids on the stoop
Would laugh
Sometimes I'd turn
Face them off
"Fuck You, "would come
Jumping out of my mouth
Just like it was supposed to.

But it's harder to say "Fuck you,"
When "Here c, c, c, comes Abraham."
Is bouncing around, inside your own head

Mrs. Chancer taught 3rd grade
She told me to slow down
Every time I'd open my mouth
She'd say, "slow down."
It drove me nuts

Mr. Wallerstein taught 5th grade
He said, "Breathe, Abe, breathe."
But none of the kids liked him
He was so spongy, talked funny
Had one eye that rolled around
And he giggled a lot
Walter put a tack on his seat
Mr. Wallerstein didn't even feel it

I sure wasn't gonna
Let him help me
But I took some deep breaths
When no one was looking

Miss Devantsis taught 7th grade
I never even heard
What she told me
I couldn't take my eyes
Off her fantastic body
Everything she had
Moved
Just like it was supposed to

In High School, Miss Giroux, my English Teacher
Did what she could
"You don't have to recite
If you don't want to."
But the part that stuck was
"You're tall
Never slouch
Stand up, straight and proud."

I wanted those cruel word games to quit
Be gone
Get lost
But they followed me through
City College Of New York

Once, In history class
The words got twisted
Broke up
Barely came out
The whole class tried not to look at me
Dr. Alston, my Professor
Called me into his office
"I'm so sorry….I didn't realize."

For four years I kept
Postponing speech class
Two lousy required credits
The final was near

You gotta give a speech

"A snap," they said
"Yeah, right." I said

Two days before the due date
Scared and panicked
I wandered into The Museum Of Modern Art
All over the place
In every room
Faces
Faces everywhere
Smiling, crying
Gazing, shocked
Scared, joyous
They called it "The Family Of Man."
I stayed all day
Bought the book
And brought it home

The prologue smashed into my soul
Carl Sandburg's wild words
Made me cry
Made me laugh
Made me say, "READ IT."

Two days later, I read it
Me and Carl Sandburg brought the house down
Professor Ramsey got up and clapped
So did the whole class

At Columbia University
The game changed some more

Professor Schwartz
Looked me in the eye
"You're damn good
You've got Social Work in your blood
In your gut
Go out there and do it."

And that's just what I did
And that's just what I do

    ****

One night, not so long ago
Rivkah and I drove to San Francisco
"The King's Speech" drew us
And then blew us away

"Fuck, fuck, fuck, fuck fuck!"
Screamed The King
"Fuck, fuck, fuck, fuck, fuck!"
Screamed I

And when the house lights came up
There was The King
Standing in the back
Waiting for Rivkah and myself

"I know you." He said
"I know you," I said

He took us to a quiet Pub
Ordered late night snacks
And their finest champagne
And we sat there, just swapping stories
And no one recognized him!

A College Christmas

The Post Office is hiring
Night work, sorting, experience preferred
Me and Andy looked at the flyer
"Experience preferred?"
We laughed
When you're in college everything's an adventure

She was there
Throwing letters into slots
Piling packages up on carts
Hauling boxes to the elevators
Stacking up sacks of mail
She was no kid
For her, this was no college adventure

When I was stuck she'd show me how
"Don't let the supervisor see you
Or you'll be in trouble
A lotta people want a job."

11 to 7 every night
She always said hello
Kept right on working
A few hours later the supervisor would swing by
And disappear for the night
Then she'd slow down
Way down
And we could see she was struggling

"You OK?"
This was job number 3
Two kids at home
Her mother is God's blessing
But she was so tired

One night, after the supervisor left
I dragged over a mail sack
"Get in."
"Oh Dios Mio, I can't do that."
Go on, get in, go to sleep."
She looked up, put her hands on my face
"You sure?"

"I'm sure, get in, go to sleep, we got it."

That Christmas Andy and I worked hard
But when you're in college everything's an adventure

School Days

"Anybody sitting here?"
Moses was holding his lunch tray
Me and Bob looked up

His hair all teased
Red rouge on his brown cheeks
Mascara hanging off his eyelashes
"No, come ahead." I said

Our high school cafeteria
A total mixed bag
But Moses Rayburn
Too much for any one bag

He'd swish down the hallway
Girls would giggle
Guys would move away
Occasionally bump him
"Oh, sorry Moses."
"Oh Moses, you dropped your lipstick."
He never stopped
Always in motion

But lunch time
Was always hard
Today Moses seemed lost
Bob and I shifted
Moses sat down

Bob was captain of the wrestling team
A big ladies man
I was president of the honor society
Lots of Bob's ladies landed in my corner
Moses was in every play
The drama club put on

"So how's it coming?" Bob chuckled
Moses looked down
I saw the welt under the red rouge
"What happened to you?"
Moses looked up
"You guys are sitting with the famous faggot!

The famous faggot who just got his ass kicked."
We all looked at each other
Didn't eat much lunch

A few days later me and Bob were walking on 8th avenue
A few blocks from school

Above the street racket
We heard it
Screams punching through the air
On the corner up ahead, there was Moses
His books scattered on the ground
Four guys surrounding him
Pushing him, getting their swings in
Their jeers laced with hate
"You faggot, faggot, black faggot."
Moses shrieking, "fuck you, fuck you!"

Suddenly, like thunder, Bob roared in
A tornado exploding down the avenue
His rage bouncing off the buildings
"You, you, you and you
You fuck with him, you fuck with me!"

And just that fast it ended
The tormentors backed off
And sulked on down the street

We reached down, gathered up the scattered books
"Here you go, Moses."
Moses took them and tucked them under his arm
He looked right as us, his eyes wet
"Thank you."

High school ended and so did we
Bob made millions selling furniture in Texas
Moses climbed onto the Off Broadway stage
I headed to California
To chase demons from peoples' minds

Forty years later my phone rang
Bob's chuckle came through
"Hey Abe, I finally tracked you down."

We visited
We tried to rekindle our fire
But our school days were over
And the force of his tornado
Had changed its course

"Send all those aliens back to Mexico."
"We need a big fence."
"Send all those ragheads back to wherever the hell they came from."
"The fags, let them live together
But they should never get married."

He went on and on
He wouldn't slow down
He drove right through my stop sign

The last time I saw him I asked
"Whatever happened to the guy
Who stood up for Moses and shouted,
'You fuck with him, you fuck with me.'"

I never got an answer

When Two Bodies Met

"Gin a body meet a body
Comin' thro' the Rye
Gin a body kiss a body,
Need a body cry?"

When they kissed there was no sadness
When they kissed they thought they were alone
But they were not
And soon the whole college knew
Two guys kissing
And the ridicule began

Need a body cry?

Did Tyler Clementi cry
As he climbed the rail of The George Washington Bridge?
Did he cry as he looked down at the swift water below?
And did he cry as he let go of his young life?

"Gin a body meet a body
Comin' thro' the glen,
Gin a body kiss a body,
Need the warld ken?"

No, the world need not know
But the world found out
And drove him to the rail on September 22nd, 2010
And Robert Burns in 1782, wondered
"If a body kiss a body,
Need a body cry?"

No More Bailing

Leonard stood in the doorway, hesitating
"Mr. Bristow wanted me to talk to you."

Gary Bristow taught science and social studies
He had an antenna that tuned into students
Who were sinking
Gary knew how to cut loose a lifeboat
Get the kid into it
And push it into calmer waters
Sometimes he'd push the boat my way

Leonard's lifeboat was leaking badly
But Leonard was too busy freaking out to bail
So I climbed on board

Many weeks later
 A lot of muddy water was gone
The bottom of the boat began to appear
We fantasized a book called, "How To Stay Afloat."
Leonard chuckled when I suggested a chapter on
How to steer a straight course
"Mr. Sass, it's a course, but it's definitely not straight."

One day he said it
"I'm scared to tell my parents
I worry about it all the time
They'll never understand."

I looked at Leonard
"You may be right
You may be wrong
You'll never know till you give it a shot
But you know
Who YOU are."
"Yeah, that's true."
"And you're done bailing a leaky boat."
"Damn right."

The following week Gary and I
Waited for Leonard
He walked in
Shut the door
Then jumped

"They didn't go nuts
They're in shock
But they didn't go crazy like I thought
They're OK with it!"

Gary reached over
Put his hand on Leonard's shoulder
"You mean they're OK with YOU!"

"Yeah, that's what I mean.

Gary brought up his hand
High Fives all around

Another 14-Year-Old-Kid

They came in together
Sat down
She looked at the floor
He reached over
Took her hand
"It's ok," He said

She lifted her head
"Mr. Bristow says you'll help."
"I will, we both will."
"I'm so scared."
She started to cry
"I'm only 14
Me and my boyfriend
We did a stupid thing."

That's how it started
"We did a stupid thing."
Two young kids
With grown up problems

Don't the kids have enough
To struggle with
Without seeing
The grotesque signs
Held up by old men
Standing in front of Planned Parenthood?

Don't the kids have enough
To struggle with
Without hearing
The angry shouts of "baby killer"

The Republican Party doesn't think so
"C'mon hop on our free shuttle bus
We'll take you to the anti abortion rally."
Yell and scream
Hold up your dirty pictures
And then hop back on
We'll take you to the National Republican Convention
We'll give you two for the price of one

In the meantime
There's a pregnant 14 year old kid
Sitting somewhere
Looking down at the floor

Who'll Take Care Of The Baby?

"My Mama said she would take care of the baby."
She sat looking at me
Black mascara
Round her eyes
Crooked and starting to drip down
Her friends had brought her over
"Go talk to him."
They pushed her in and disappeared

At first she wore baggy clothes
But now everyone could see
"Man, that girl, she got knocked up big time."
Going down the hall was an obstacle course
She didn't know what to do
So she let them push her in

But whatever we talked about
And the many ways we turned it all about
It was no match for her Mama saying
"Don't you worry, I'll take care of the baby."

And when I met Mama
Mama said it to me
"Don't worry, I'll take care of the baby."
Signed and sealed
So she dropped out of high school
And out of sight

And then one day
She was there
A wreck
Mama was gone
Off on a meth-charged flight
And "I'll take care of the baby"
Was a sad echo

Child Protective Services
Was Mama now
And the mascara was still crooked
And starting to drip down

August 28th, 1963

The sun glares down on us
The heat so intense
And now, another person has fainted
This time it's a woman
She was holding up a sign

WE
DEMAND
EQUAL RIGHTS
NOW!

She's being lifted up
By all of us
We who today
Have become one loving family

We hold her high in the air
Many hands
Gently
Tenderly
"Got her?"
"Yeah, keep her comin'."

We slowly pass her over our heads
Toward the side
Where the medics wait to help
"You're gonna be fine now."

We are the sea
We cradle her softly, safely
On our calm waters

And her sign is now held high
By a new family member

We came from all over
Cars, buses, trains
Faces grinning from passing windows
Hands waving
Lights flashing
Electricity snapping in the morning air

As we enter Washington
The sun is coming up
All the bathrooms are full
Peein'
Washin' up
Changin' clothes
Gettin' there
Lookin' good

Gathering at The Washington Monument
"We're from New York."
"We're up from Tennessee."
"We been on the road four days."
"Our whole congregation's here."
"Seems everybody's headin' this way."
"Never saw so many people in all my life."

As the singing begins
A guy wearing a straw hat touches my shoulder
Smiles at me
"Glorious day!" He says
I smile back
"The very best!"
We reach out
We join hands
Our heads lift up
Our voices swell, swell to the clear blue of the sky

"WE SHALL OVERCOME, WE SHALL OVERCOME
WE SHALL OVERCOME SOMEDAY
OH DEEP IN MY HEART, I DO BELIEVE
WE SHALL OVERCOME SOMEDAY."

Slowly we all begin to march
Steady, proud, united
We raise our signs high
Many of us reach over and hold our neighbor's hand
Even the birds flying so high above, they know
They know that this is no ordinary day in Washington DC

At The Lincoln Memorial
We stand close to each other
In the midday heat
Listening to those whose names are legends
Whose deeds have changed the world
Folks who have put their souls on the line
They all reach out to us
They touch us
A touch I will always remember

And when HE shares HIS dream
We who stand in awe
Are brought on board The Freedom Train

My tall body lets me see far above everyone
I see all of us
Stretching from The Lincoln Memorial
Out over the whole city
Out over the whole country
Out over the whole world

But never so far away
That I will ever forget
How on that hot day
We all reached up
To gently, tenderly, support those of us
Who could stand up no longer

Organic Carrot Juice

She stands behind a little table at Costco
One of many women
Cutting and pouring samples
"Organic carrot juice
High in antioxidants."

She's near the back
Not much traffic coming her way
"How you folks doing today?"
"Just fine, thanks."

My wife Rivkah and I stop for some healthy refreshment
To wash down the chips and cheese and sausages

"This carrot juice is organic
Real high in antioxidants."
She pours, smiles
"Thank you, it's real good."
She pours some more
And goes on about those antioxidants

Suddenly, in mid stream, she stops
She leans forward to me
A small gasp
She leans closer
She is looking at the button
Pinned to my bib overalls

Black and white hands
Clasped together
MARCH ON WASHINGTON
FOR JOBS AND FREEDOM
AUGUST 28, 1963

She looks up at me
"Were you there?"
"Yes I was."
"You were really there?"
I smile
"Oh yes, I was there."

"Oh my god, you were there"
"Oh my god, you were there."
Her eyes glisten
"Oh…please, tell me."

As the three of us go on a journey together
Back to the magic of that day
Tears roll down her soft brown cheeks
She reaches out
Takes my hands in hers

Brown and white hands
Clasped together
Above the bottles
Of organic carrot juice

Jury Duty, 2013

I swear, I never knew
The assistant District Attorney could dance

Every time he asked the white folks
Sitting in the jury box
"Can you be fair and impartial in this case?"
He just stood there
Glued to his favorite spot
As one by one they all said "yes."

Every once in a while
He'd glance over at the defendant
A young, black man

Then he came to you
I guess he figured
Because you're a young black woman
You've got a good sense of rhythm

So he loosened up
Moved from his favorite spot
Did a little soft shoe number
And then he pulled some sweet talk right out of the air
And laid it right on you

You looked right at him
And said, "Yes, it bothers me
That our prisons house so many black men
But I can examine the evidence
And be a fair and impartial juror."

I watched him smile
Move on back to his favorite spot
And write some notes on his paper

Later, the judge read that paper
And turned to you
"Thank you for your service
You're excused."

You stood up
Looked at everyone in that courtroom
Picked up your purse
And slowly walked out

When it was all over
I walked home
Through Cesar Chavez park

It felt like you were right there
Walking next to me
Holding up that 50 year old sign

WE
DEMAND
EQUAL RIGHTS
NOW!

Me and Frank

A white guy from New York City
A Black guy from San Rafael
A couple of exorcists
Driving out the demons at
Napa State Hospital in the sixties

Let's go to lunch, I hear there's a place down the road
You ever been there?
Nope
Let's try it

So we went on over and we ordered
And we sat there
The people came in and ate
We kept sitting there
"We're out of what you ordered."
"That's ok, we'll order something else."
"We're out of anything you order."

Two days later I came back
Our whole CORE chapter and Frank
We sat there all day
Pretty much filled the place
We sat there the next day

None of us said much except
"We're not moving till we get served."
The white folks couldn't sit down
All the tables were filled
Mostly with Black folks
All hungry for some Napa County white bread food

On day three we ate

Every once in a while
Me and Frank would drop on by
Just to smile, say hello, ready to perform another exorcism
Then we'd drive on back to the looney bin
But we knew by then
The real loonies are not in the bin

She Sang

Madame Mayor, will you join us in singing "We Shall Overcome?"
She looked up at me
"Who are we overcoming?" she asked with a twinkle in her eye
"The bad guys," I answered
She smiled, "Indeed."
I reached out, she took my hand, and she sang

And all the people who had gathered
Sang with her
Voices strong
Voices urgent
People who needed to be heard
People who had come
To stop the wrecking ball
From breaking up their homes

"New houses
Better houses
Affordable houses."

The developers sold that hype
But everyone knew the truth
Luxury condos and high prices were down the road

Herb Caen heard the story
Wrote it up
"The Mayor joins hands
With the CORE Freedom Schoolers
To sing "We Shall Overcome."

She was a little woman
She took a big step
She took a lot of flack
For singing that song

I still remember how tiny her hand seemed in mine
I still remember her voice rising up
And I hope she kept that twinkle in her eye

Martin

He was the man who had a dream
He told the world about it
People came and joined him

For a few short years
People turned to him
For a few short years
People called on him to lead the cause
People marched and prayed
Sang, sat down, and went to jail

People took the clubbings, the dogs
The fire hoses, the burnings
The bullets and the hate
Took it all to make a better world
And he was there, always

On April 4th, 1967, at Riverside Church in New York City
Martin speaks out with a different voice
He pleads for The United States to end its assault on Vietnam
He is clear
It is an assault
And it diminishes all of us
"A nation that continues year after year to spend more money on
military defense than on programs of social uplift is approaching
spiritual death," he says

People who were with him turned away
People who he counted on turned him down
Newspaper editorials tore him up
Stick to civil rights, they said
Leave Vietnam alone

But he didn't, he wouldn't
He told the truth until April 4th, 1968
The day that bullet cut him down

My Mother's Words

"I get a dollar a dress, " says my mother

She punches the time clock
Goes to her sewing machine
On a long line of sewing machines
She joins a long line of women
Bent over, pushing the cloth through
In a sweat shop
In the garment district in New York City

"I get thirty minutes for lunch."

She shoves the unfinished dresses to the side
Makes a little space
For her egg salad sandwich

"I get a bathroom break
But I've learned to make it quick
Or the bosses make your life miserable."

One evening, after supper
She turns to me
"No one should have to work in a sweat shop."

My mother's words
Bounced off the sweat shop walls
At Tazreen Fashions, in Bangladesh in 2012
As the long lines of women
Tumbled to the locked doors
Pounding, screaming
Smoke and flames assaulting them

My mother's words
Bounced off the sweat shop walls
At The Triangle Shirtwaist Company, in New York in 1911
As the long lines of women
Tumbled to the locked doors
Pounding, screaming
Smoke and flames assaulting them

In New York
And so many years later
In Bangladesh
When the doors stood firm
Locked tight
The windows beckoned

The women in their terror
Crashed through
Gasping, screaming
Wounded birds
Plunging to the concrete below

Now, like then
We wear our clothes with style
Now, like then
We shudder at the photographs
And create committees

But the long lines of women
Still sit, bent over their sewing machines
Pushing the cloth through

My Mother's Ghost

They're changing the name
No more garment district in New York City
It's now called The Fashion Plaza
And the women in my mother's time
Who toiled in sweatshops
And gave their all
Are gone

But cheap clothes
Are still here

So we're outsourcing the sweat shops

Those long lines of women
Bent over their sewing machines
They've all hopped the subway
To Bangladesh!

Climb on the downtown local
As it rumbles through
Tunnels
Crosses bridges
Shrieks through time and place

The women on the subway squeeze together
Cling to the handrails

Leaning against the door
Two women face each other
"I heard they found big cracks in the building
Just yesterday."

"Yes, but the boss says not to worry."

The subway rumbles on
Wheels squeal
As the overloaded cars
Swing round a curve

The subway enters the station
The loudspeaker crackles
"Rana Plaza, Garment District."
The doors slide open
The women tumble out

" I want to see those cracks."
"We're late. We'll see them
After work."

Five floors of sweat shops fill up
Women take their places
Sewing machines crank up
No one hears the building groan
No one hears the cracks split wide open

As the sewing machines clatter
The building erupts
Roars
Concrete not worth a damn
Collapsing
Crushing
Smashing
Tearing

Mothers, daughters
Trapped in Hell
Skewered
Severed
Ripped apart

As the horror travels round the world
Day after day
Night after night
They pull the bodies out

 200 and counting
 800 and counting
1000 and still counting
The bloody arithmetic goes on

But the Subways keep running
The downtown local
Still rumbles through tunnels
Still crosses bridges
Still shrieks through time and place

The women
Still squeeze together
And cling to the handrail
As the subways
Still travel to more sweatshops
In new and exotic cities

Now, like then
We wear our clothes with style
Now, like then
We shudder at the photographs
And we create committees

But in sweat shops round the world
The long lines of women
Still sit, bent over their sewing machines
Pushing the cloth through

And my mother's ghost cries out
"No one should have to work in a sweat shop."

Pete Seeger

You walk slowly now, your canes steady you
No banjo slung from your shoulder
Your voice is now a rough whisper
How is it your voice can still rise above a crowd?
How is it your songs still ring, so true?

You look up and all around
And this is what you see
Faces of then, faces of now
Shining eyes lighting your path

You turn your head to catch the singing
And this is what you hear
Voices of then, voices of now
Still singing your songs, so true

"Oh, I can hardly hear you!"
You swing your arm up
Holding us in your open palm
And we all sing louder

One night, long ago, my mother and I
Were on 8th street in Greenwich Village
We saw you slowly walking up the block
Alone
Your banjo tucked into its big black case
Slung from your shoulder

My mother stopped you
"I'm Sylvia
We met at the Yugoslav-American home
You were singing with Paul Robeson."
You smiled
And then your eyes brightened
"Say, why don't you both join me
At a house concert
It's just up the block here."

The apartment was packed
But you found a chair for my mom
I sat on the floor
My eyes wide with wonder

You pulled your banjo out
Its round skin proudly announcing
"This machine surrounds hate
And forces it to surrender"

Then you looked over at my mom
And down at me
"Let me introduce you
To friends of mine
Sylvia and her son Abraham
She's a garment worker
And part of the struggle for worker's rights."

Then you started to play
Then you started to sing
Then you did what you always do
You got us all singing together
And my wonder turned to joy

> "So who's your hero?" asked Rivkah
> As we approached the Golden Gate Bridge in 1976
> "Pete Seeger."
> She smiled, "Great choice!"
> "So, who's yours?"
> "Daniel Ellsberg."
> I smiled, "Great choice!"
>
> And later that day, in San Francisco
> We saw Daniel Ellsberg eating his ice cream
> A totally awed Rivkah approached and said,"You're my
> hero!"
> His hug enveloped her
> And later I told him who my choice was
> He laughed
> "Well, if I'm with Pete Seeger
> I'm in good company."
> As his hug enveloped me

We joined Pete at Madison Square Garden
To celebrate his 90th birthday

He looked up and all around
And this is what he saw
Faces of then
Faces of now
Shining eyes lighting his path

And as he turned his head to catch the singing
This is what he heard
Voices of then
Voices of now
Still singing his songs, so true

And when he swung his arm up
Holding us in his open palm
We all sang louder
As we have for all these years

Pete Seeger died in January of 2014
He still sings in my heart
He's still my hero

Sister Megan Rice

Hey Sister Megan Rice
Where are you going with those fence cutters?
"Getting through the fence at Oak Ridge
Where they store the enriched uranium."

Hey Sister Megan Rice
What are you doing with that spray can?
"Painting messages of peace and love on the walls."

Hey Sister Megan Rice
What are you doing with all that food?
"Giving it to the police as they arrest me."

Hey sister Megan Rice
What are you singing as they arrest you?
"Songs of peace, songs of love."

Hey Sister Megan Rice
The judge said three years for you
"Well, I'm eighty four, three more makes eighty seven
Think they'll have room for me in heaven?"

Hey Sister Megan Rice
If you get there before I do
Say Hello to Pete Seeger
He'll sing a song of peace and love for you

Another Flight Over The Cuckoo's Nest

He had a mouthful of crooked teeth
He had a twisty crooked walk
But he carried his shoe shine box everywhere he went
And he went everywhere
Into offices, on the lawn, behind the buildings
Of the Mental Hospital
"You need a shine, hey you, you need a shine,
I'll shine 'em up for you."

But sometimes he'd fall
And hit his head
So they made him wear a helmet
And he'd take off the helmet
"I don't need that helmet," he said
"But sometimes you fall," they said
"So I fall," he said
"My head is still here!"

And everyone he'd meet
And everyone he'd greet
They all had shiny feet
And his head never disappeared

But then Big Nurse came along
And decided it was time
"No more shoe shine box," she said

Then he slowly crawled inside his head
Dragons came to freak him out
Fire came to burn him out
Voices came to shout him out
His shoe shine box kept the monsters away
Kept him safe every day

Big Nurse tuned out all I said
Blew me off
Just shook her head

On Friday I stopped her
Walking on the ward
"Read this book, " I said
"It's right up your alley
You won't get bored."

On Monday she came back to me
With fury in her face
But she also carried a sad disgrace

She tried to keep up her charade
But we stopped dancing to her parade

She gave him back his shoe shine box
He smiled and took it everywhere
"You need a shine, hey you, you need a shine,
I'll shine 'em up for you."

And everyone he'd meet
And everyone he'd greet
They all had shiny feet
And his head never disappeared

Beginning

She fled Tulsa for San Francisco
They found her under a bush
Her arms cut open
They stitched her up
Sent her to the psych ward

Each week she'd come to my group
Ten fractured souls
Working to glue their pieces together
She'd sit
Watch
She never opened her door

The darkness in her eyes
Spilled out into the room
Pooled up on the floor
Thick and deep

The quiet boy
Who sat across from her in the group
Got up one day
Walked across the circle
All eyes followed him

He kneeled
Took her hands in his
Looked up at her face

"If they hadn't cut me down
I'd be dead
I been where you been
I don't want to go back
Do you?"

She slowly looked down at him
A small candle glow
Flickered behind her eyes
She shook her head
"No," she said
Every one in the group clapped

Donatella

"Donatella's up on that roof
She says she's gonna jump off."

Earlier the cops leaned a ladder
Up against the wall
And tried going up
But she screamed at them
And she knows how to scream

So I get the call
It's the middle of the night

Now the cops are leaning
Up against their car
And the ladder's still there
The cops shake their heads
Smile at me and point to the ladder
They don't know
I'm really scared of heights

"Donatella, I'm coming up."
"Don't bother."
"Donatella, I'm coming up."

I don't recognize my own voice
As I grab the ladder
My feet are shaking
My hands are shaking
And I feel the ladder shaking

Donatella's on the edge of the roof
I look straight up at her
I'm too scared to look down
She's looking right at me
As I climb up

I swing my butt
Onto the roof
She stares at me
As I scoot over towards her
"You almost fell offa that ladder."

104

"Please Donatella, don't remind me,
I'm really scared of heights."
"Ha, you're very funny."
"Not really
My wife says I've got
No sense of humor."
"Ha, And you can't climb either!"
"Like I said Donatella,
 Please don't remind me
I'm scared of high places."

We're looking right at each other
I don't know why
We both start to laugh

And then she starts to cry

"I just wanna die. I just wanna die."
"I know you do Donatella.
I know you do."

And there we are
Up on the roof
In the middle of the night
Me and Donatella
Just talking
And the cops
Still leaning on their car

Later on I reach my hand over
She reaches her hand over
"OK?" I ask
"Yeah OK."
And we both
Start to climb down that ladder

Suddenly Donatella laughs
"Hey, you're a lot better going down."

"Like I said, Donatella,
Please don't remind me.
I'm really scared of heights."

Take A Good Look

I can't take my eyes off his scar
Swirls of brown and black
Mixed with bubbles of rust
A mad canvas in motion
All screaming
Running down the side of his face
Down his neck
Disappearing under his shirt

But he's here, worried about his daughter
And he's telling me everything
And I don't hear a word

He's telling me everything
And I don't hear a word
I must tell him

And I do

He just looks at me
Looks long
Looks hard

Afraid of what I've opened, I wait

He drags his chair over
He sits right in front of me
"Take a good look."

And I do

"Do you want to know?"

"Yes."

I get on board and he takes me to another world
Into the jungles of Vietnam
He shows me nights and days of horror
Then, when I can take no more
He pulls the curtain wide open
And introduces me to Mr. Agent Orange
Who stands there, grinning in his cloak of pain and death

"Now, take another good look
And see everything that he left me with."

And I do

He pulls his shirt collar down, way down
He pulls me down, way down
I gasp, rage rising in my belly

He tells me how he has knocked on all the doors
Mailed all the letters
Made all the phone calls
And all the USA gives him are official denials and outright lies

But today all he wants
Is help to fix his daughter

And so we set out on that road

Later on, his daughter joins us
And together we do a pretty good job

Years later the truth came out
The USA had hidden Mr. Agent Orange
Behind that curtain
Telling everybody it wasn't him
And he escaped, leaving behind his maimed victims

Today they still come back, from Iraq, from Afghanistan
They knock on all the doors
Mail all the letters
Make all the phone calls
They're put on hold
Told to wait
And they are still waiting
While the USA still issues official denials and outright lies

Finally

I watched her dig the hole
She used her shovel
The one left over from when
She was a kid
It was bright blue
With yellow flowers on the handle

She's no kid now
She's got her own kid
But still her father's ghost
Keeps raping her

And for all these years
She's kept her terrible secret

Today she's digging a hole
To bury her father's ghost
So she can live

"It's got to be bigger
It's got to be deeper," she cries
Sweat breaking over her face

It's hard to dig a big hole
With a little shovel
But it's her shovel
And she's doing it

"There, now it's big enough
What do you think?"
I look down, then at her
"Yes, I think it's big enough."

She reaches into her pocket
Pulls out his faded photograph
Throws it into the hole
She looks down
"Finally I'm burying you
You can't haunt me anymore."

I thought of her today
As I read about Emma Sulkowicz
At Columbia University
She carries the mattress of her rape
Everywhere on campus
And she won't keep silent

Maybe someday
She'll bury it
Maybe someday her nightmare can end

Ms. Sulkowicz graduated Columbia in June 2015.
She carried her mattress on to the stage.
The President of Columbia declined to shake her hand.

The "I Can't Keep It In" Group

"I'm not going outside," Claire said
She was skinny, 32 years old
Her blonde hair hid her frightened eyes

Claire spent years
Running away from
School
Home
Friends
Her marriage

Her husband Tom, frustrated
Tried all he could to help her
Nothing worked

She'd scream
Cry
Shout
Curse him

Monsters had chased her
Through hallways and streets
Of San Francisco
Wherever she went they followed
Always right behind her
Never giving her time to rest

Finally, they followed her up the stairs
To her apartment
Until she just stayed put
Locked the door and wouldn't go outside

So the cops came for her
Drove her up to The Mental Hospital in Napa

My group met twice a week
Sometimes more
We called it "The I Can't Keep It In" group
"I'll come to your group," Claire told me
"But I'm not going outside."

One day they brought a new patient to the hospital
He was Native American, Chehalis
Came down to San Francisco from Seattle
Called himself River
Took too much LSD
Too much peyote
Too much everything

After his swirling flight slowed down
After he crash landed
He came to the group
Mostly listened

One day he got up, looked at Claire
"Hey Claire, you ever tell those monsters to fuck off?
You ever turn around and tell them you're busy?"

That was day one
Soon everybody got on board

Days later we were all running around the room
All stopping, all turning around
Looking right at our monsters

We drew our monsters
Acted them out
We were growling and screaming
Tacking monster pictures up on the wall
Then we'd turn and tell them to Fuck Off

Claire's husband Tom visited her two months later
She was prepared
"I'm not keeping it in any longer."
She walked to everyone in the group
Hugged us all
She gave a long, special hug to River
He touched her hair
"Go outside with God and your husband."
We watched as Claire and Tom
Walked towards the door
She took Tom's arm
And they both walked outside

Concertina Wire

It catches the sun's rays
Swirls them up and around
A dance
So graceful to see
So sinister in its purpose

The concertina wire is new at the mental hospital
It sits on a high brick fence
A fence so high
Even Batman couldn't break out

The crazy people locked behind the fence
Have all gone astray
Their forest has become dark, overgrown

We who try to mend these
Broken people
We wonder
"Are the new crazy people
Crazier than those who came here before?
Have the walls become not tall enough?
Is concertina wire the answer?"

And if you are a crazy Batman
Or a crazy Nowhere Man
When you look up
And see that concertina wire
Would it not make you crazier?

How dare they call it concertina!
Some of the old men in my growing up neighborhood
Played concertinas
The music would come pulsing out as they squeezed them
They would sing as they strolled down the block
People would smile
Toss a coin or two
An aria

This Ain't The Fabulous Forties

The Sacramento Dancer

She holds up the dress
A lucky find
It may even fit
She grips it by the shoulders
And gently sways it
From side to side
She smiles and watches it flutter

Then she drapes it round her body
One hand holds the dress
Above her breasts
The other hand gathers the dress
Against her waist

Slowly, to some inner music
She begins to swing her hips
Then twirls round and round
She kicks up one leg
Then the other
The dress clings to her
She turns in a graceful arc
And then, slowly
Ever so slowly
Takes a long sweeping bow

The people walking by the doorway
Gaze over
They see her rusty shopping cart
Piled high with pieces of her life
They see her face
Grime smeared
A smattering of lipstick
A swollen eye
And they keep walking

Ah, but they missed the dance
When the spotlight caught her
Followed her across the stage

And they never had the chance
To stand and shout, "Bravo!"

Bus Stops

No line waiting
It's just me on a bright Sacramento day
Heading downtown
The big bus pulls up
The door swings open

"I've got my senior card
I've got my buck and a quarter
And I'm ready for anything."

The bus driver laughs at me
Bright eyes
A salt and pepper beard and mustache
"Well, looks like you are..
Hop on up for the best ride in town!"

I slide into my seat
In the seat behind me
Two little old ladies
Are deep into their conversation

"You gotta get the dough just right."
"I never can."
"You gotta add oil to your dough or It'll dry out."
"Oil?"
"Yes, oil."
"You add nuts?"
"Of course."
"What kinda nuts you add?"
"Walnuts."

The cooking channel on the number 30 bus
No commercials
Just straight programming from the seat behind me

Next Stop

The bus bows down
 A lady pushes a well worn stroller up onto the step
Shoves it over to the side
Her face thin, her expression a struggle

She holds an infant to her chest, reaches down
Grabs a crying little girl, pulls her up, grunts

With her hands full she turns again
Up come two more kids
A big brother, maybe six years old
Dragging his little sister up
The mother clutches her infant
Pulls the little crying girl up next to her on the bench seat
Big brother squeezes in next to them
Leaving just enough space for little sister

The mother digs into her bag for her bus card
The driver sees her struggle
"That's ok," he says, " I know you got it."
She keeps on digging
Pulls out the bus card, holds it up
"You got it, hang on, off we go."
He gives her a great salt and pepper grin
As he turns and grips the big steering wheel

I watch big brother oodle and coo his sister
I watch the mother hold and hug her infant
I watch the crying girl snuggle close to mom
Pops her thumb in her mouth
"Your son is sure a great helper," I say
The mother looks at me
"He's a good son."
"I believe it'"

We travel on
A few blocks further the mother's head starts to nod
Soon she's asleep, clutching her infant
The rest of the family sitting so quiet
The crying girl is enjoying her thumb

From the seat behind me the cooking channel
Is done baking
Now they're making pot roast

Next Stop

The driver swings close to the curb
The bus hisses as it lowers itself
A woman slowly, painfully, struggles up the steps
She's enormous
Wheezing so loud it shocks
She's dragging a little boy
"Need any help, lady?"
The driver starts to move from his seat
She shakes her head, "No," she says
She struggles on
Finally sits
Taking up two seats

Her boy is wedged against the window
He twists around, stares at the man sitting behind him
The man starts to fidget
The boy keeps staring right at him
The man looks away
The boy just stares

And from the kitchen, in the seat behind me
Onions and celery are being chopped
And now they're adding lots of garlic
I can smell the pot roast simmering

Next Stop

"There is a gentleman up ahead who is blind
 Please make some room up here in the front."
The driver pulls the bus over
The front dips down
The man comes up
He is dressed in a sharp cut suit, crisp shirt, bright tie
His service dog is a brown Labrador
With gentle eyes
The driver is off his chair
"Here sir."

120

He guides them to the seat

"Thank you." The man tips his head up and smiles
His Lab curls up between his legs
"My pleasure sir."
As the driver walks back to his seat he turns
"Everybody here ok?"
His salt and pepper smile touches everyone

The enormous woman slowly nods off
Her wheezing now is slight
The staring boy keeps right on staring
At the man behind him

The mother has woken up, she smiles
Big brother seems fine
The little girl keeps right on sucking her thumb

The cooking channel ladies
Have served up their pot roast
And now they're swapping chicken soup secrets

I stand as my stop comes up
As I step down I turn to Mister Salt and Pepper Bus Driver
"You are so right, this IS the best ride in town!"
He laughs, "I told you so."

Midwives Hold The Future In Their Hands

"Midwives Hold The Future In Their Hands"
A simple license plate frame
And it caught me
Made me stop
Made me turn my head around
Half expecting to see
My son and daughter
Coming down the street to me

One shining star dancing in the cosmos
One shining star dancing here on earth

And we who love these shining stars
And we who love these fragile faces
Soon come to know
That life takes the future where it will

But some of us will always remember
The midwives who gently hold the future in their hands
A simple license plate frame
And it caught me
Made me stop
Made me turn my head around

California Crops

I pull the wheel sharply
Feel the car hug the turn
It's tight, flat
No sway, no letting go
The huge sliding roof
Wide open
Sucking in the breeze

Below the road
The ocean
Rolling over slick, black coast rocks
White foam swirling
I inhale it all

As the road zig-zags
Lush green fields appear
"What's growing?" I shout
Against the glorious breeze
Rivkah points and yells
"Artichokes!"
We zig
"Cabbages."
We zag
"Lettuce."
She's got California farmer's daughter's blood
I've got New York garment worker's son's blood

As we come round a curve
Another long, wide field stretches out
We see a different crop
Faded shades of orange, purple and brown
Shirts
Shirts on stooped backs
Shirts soaked in sweat
Spread out in the field
Slowly moving
Stark against the lush green

The dusty trucks and honey buckets appear
All clustered near the makeshift platforms
And the all important scales

I hear the voices in my head
"How much per pound today?"
"How much per sack today?"
"How much for a bent back today?"

We've just come from John Steinbeck's Museum
I've got his Dubious Battle and his Harvest Gypsies
Coursing through me
And suddenly here they are
Michoacan browns
Not Oklahoma whites
But that's the only difference
The work still kills

The need to grind up a person
To turn a profit
Still sits heavy on the
Artichokes
Cabbages
And lettuce

And as I pull into another curve
I wish for another John Steinbeck
And another Cesar Chavez
And another Jose Montoya

Watermelon Men

For Rivkah's father

We were walking side by side
Out in the "back 40."
FonSeca's guys had picked the watermelons
We were hunting for the dusty leftovers

Poppa, in his bibs, bent down, scooped one up
Out came his blue handled knife
And the watermelon cracked wide open
He sliced into it
Some for him
Some for me
Juice ran down our chins
We laughed and tossed the pieces high in the air
They made little dust clouds when they hit
On we went
Scooping, cutting, cracking, eating and laughing
And flinging the pieces high in the air!

Later, after dinner, Grandma served cold watermelon slices
Poppa and I Just looked at each other and smiled
We both knew
There was nothing could compare
To walking in the "back 40"
Cracking open those watermelons
Some for him
Some for me
And flinging the pieces high in the air!

A Popping Sound

As I wait for the green light
Rivkah's dad sits in the passenger's seat
Staring out the window
At the two EMTs on the corner
Helping a man into an ambulance
On a clear, sunny, Portland day

The light changes
As we enter the intersection
Poppa turns his head
Still staring at the scene on the corner

"Abe, pull over."
His voice is shaking
His hand slides over, grips my knee

I see a spot and make for it
He turns to me
"It was a popping sound
Just a popping sound I heard."
I turn off the motor
His face is flushed
"Poppa, what's happening?"

He looks down
His right hand comes up
Covers his eyes
His left hand grabs mine
Holds on tight, so tight

"That day, oh, that day."
He slowly looks up
Loosens his grip
"Poppa, can you tell me?"

He takes me to a Pacific Island in World War 2
He's landed Marines in his Higgens Boat
Tbey're advancing up the beach
His good buddy is next to him

"It was a popping sound
Just a popping sound I heard

And I turned to him
And he's falling all backwards
But his head's all blown away
There's pieces still in the air."

For a long time we sit there
As my father-in-law
Slowly comes back
From that terrible moment
On a Pacific Island
To Portland, Oregon
On a clear, sunny, day

Amazing Grace

When the Sacramento summer midday heat
Begins its slow swan song
Capitol Park whispers in my ear

"Come on
Walk over
I'm here for you."

As I enter the park
A swirling, wailing sound
Comes slicing through the air
Pulling me in
Toward a lush grove of trees

A large group of bagpipers
Are standing, playing, facing each other
In a vast circle

In the center of the circle
3 drummers drive a steady beat

The music pulses out
Flies up
Wraps itself around the trees
Then swoops down
And gently caresses
The sculpted, anguished face
Of the lone fireman
Who carries his mortally wounded comrade

As I stand, watching, listening
I remember the lone bagpiper
Who stood in the rain
As Rivkah's father was laid to rest
And I hear the wail and the cry
Of the holy music
As it gently caressed all our faces

Another Road Trip

For Rivkah

The moon and stars
A bright sun
Hills, towns, meadows and streams
All stitched onto the ceiling
Of our red VW bus

Rivkah's art work looking down
On the fold out bed
We sleep on
Love on
Eat on
Play scrabble on
As we meander from Santa Rosa, California
To Rivkah's cousins in Storm Lake, Iowa
To my mother in New York City, in 1976

Tucked under the bed
Imported from Rivkah's folks' farm
Manteca's watermelon harvest
And as we round a curve
Rolling across the floor
Manteca's watermelon harvest

In Storm Lake
The welcome mat is out for us
"That's your Cousin Louie!"
Rivkah's Aunt points to the scrapbook
Cousin Louie is laying in his coffin
"And there's his wife, Sarah"
Cousin Sarah is laying in her coffin

Page after page
Cousin after cousin
Everybody's laying out in their coffins
In their "going to church" clothes
"An old Danish tradition," they say

I'm looking for the door
Rivkah pats my shoulder
Smiles
"Just go with it."

The next day
We're high up in the cab
Of Rivkah's Uncle's giant combine
Its powerful arms stretched out
Cutting and baling long sharp rows
In a sea of corn
I'm wearing my bib overalls
Playing farmer
Rivkah's Uncle turns to me and says
"You want to drive her?"
"Oh, you bet!"

A few moments later
He moves me gently aside
"I think I better do it."
His polite midwest style
Helps me realize
I need to stick to driving
Our red VW bus

Cut That Wheel Just Right

For Ilana

I watched you
Move that catering truck on out
Back it toward the gate
Big, lumbering, clunking thing
Been around the block a lot

I watched the side mirror catch you
Looking
This way than that
I sucked my breath in
As the gate post got real close
But you cut that wheel just right

I've been there before
Watching you
Sucking my breath in

"I wanna take the city bus myself."
You know I didn't want you to do it
But you've always had a way
To make me say
"OK."
So I held my breath
Sucked it in
And watched you hop that city bus
As you went off to 3rd grade

You're still hoppin'
I'm still watchin'
But now you got the wheel
So watch out for those gate posts
And cut that wheel just right!

This Ain't The Fabulous Forties

He's hunched over, twisted
Huddled in the corner doorway
A straight tight line of mouth
Cuts across the roadmap of his face
His hands are jammed into the pockets of his raggedy coat
His eyes peer out from under his watch cap
They fix on the red traffic light just ahead

The light turns green
People begin to cross
He steps out from the doorway
Slow, stiff shuffles
He moves toward the curb
Slow, stiff shuffles

The people have all crossed
He continues straight ahead
The light turns red
He doesn't stop
He steps down into the street

Brakes screech
Cars shudder, then stop
People turn and stare
"Hey man, you wanna get killed?"
"For chrissakes buddy, you nuts?"

Now he uncoils
Now he unhunches
He bolts upright
His eyes flash
His head snaps up
His hands flip up
His legs jump up
He is out on the street
Twirling wildly

The people suddenly erupt
"YO, MAN, DO IT! DO IT!"
"GO FOR IT! YEAH!"

His mouth opens wide
He roars
He laughs
He leaps high in the air
Spinning madly

He comes to the curb
Leaps up, up onto the sidewalk
He stops

The cars slowly start up
The people move on
Some turn, look back, watch him

He jams his hands into the pockets of his raggedy coat
He hunches over
A straight, tight line of mouth
Cuts across the roadmap of his face

He moves off
Slow, stiff shuffles

Sanctuary

The morning heat is laying low
As I come to the church on 13th Street and Capitol Park
Heading to a gathering at Rivkah's library

The big bundle in the doorway
Of the church
Catches my eye
I stop, turn and look
The man is all curled up
Under a raggedy coat

A few bags of stuff
Shoved in the corner
Make for a pillow
A trickle of wetness
Follows the crack in the sidewalk
Down to the curb

I look over at Capitol park
All lush and green
This is no cracked tenement block
Like my growing up one
In New York City

But I know this man
Under the raggedy coat
I know him well

I'm back in New York
Walking past Delgado's candy store
Locked up for the night
Heading down West 18th street
Coming home late
After a long evening
At Shep's house
Helping him with his
Bar Mitzvah lessons
Two weeks after my Bar Mitzvah

The big bundle
In the doorway
Of the cracked tenement

Catches my eye
I stop, turn and look
The man is all curled up
Under a raggedy coat

A few bags of stuff
Shoved in the corner
Make for a pillow
A trickle of wetness
Follows the crack in the sidewalk
Down to the curb

West 18th Street
New York City
13th Street
Sacramento
Same scene
Same wetness
Trickling down to the curb

"You said he's in the church doorway?" the 311 worker asked
"Yes," I said
"Can you stay at the church till the ambulance gets there?"
"Yes, I'll stay with him
There's times when we all need sanctuary."

That Same Cop

Thungk, thungk, thungk

It was a dense, deep sound

It came at me just as I turned the corner of 18th Street
Coming home late
Still reliving the party at Shep's house
Celebrating our 13th birthdays

Thungk, thungk, "no, no, noooooo."

In the doorway, I see them
The cop, whomping his fist into the kid
Me, stuck, frozen
Fright roaring through my body
I see the kid's nose, mouth, all blood
"Noooo, please, noooo!"
The cop raises his fist again
Then stops, turns
His eyes hit me, hard
"Go on, get outta here!"
I run home

But I saw his face
The same cop who smiles at the old people
Who sit on wooden boxes and folding chairs
On the corner of West 18th Street and 8th Avenue
That same cop

Shrapp, shrapp, shrapp, shrapp, shrapp, shrapp, shrapp

The sound of their boots bounces off the buildings
The dark night throws shadows along Telegraph Avenue
The soldiers are marching toward UC Berkeley
Each one carries a rifle
On each rifle, horrifying as the street lamps catch their glint
Is a bayonet

I watch
My late night walk, now a scene from Twilight Zone
But there is no soothing Rod Serling
Just armed soldiers on a frightening mission
And standing in the street
Cops
All dressed for mayhem

As the soldiers march by
One cop raises his fist high
Shouts out, "Go on, give it to 'em!"

But I saw his face
The same cop who smiles at the old people
Who sit on wooden boxes and folding chairs
On the corner of West 18th Street and 8th Avenue
That same cop

"Shame on you, shame on you, shame on you."

The students at UC Davis chant
As they're pepper sprayed by the cops

"Shame on you, shame on you, shame on you."

The students chant
As they're dragged off by the cops

"Shame on you, shame on you, shame on you."

But the cameras are here, the cell phones are here
And from UC Davis, it all goes out
Round the world
All in bright, bright, daylight

And I see him
Yes, I see his face under his riot mask
The same cop who smiles at the old people
Who sit on wooden boxes and folding chairs
On the corner of 18th Street and 8th Avenue
That same cop

Loosies

Old man Delgado used to sell loosies
To all the kids in my neighborhood
Kept them in a cup under the counter
Two loose cigarettes for a nickel

Everybody knew it
Even the cops
They always got their sodas
From old man Delgado
That was light years ago

Now "loosies" are sold all over
Even on the street
But if you're Black, in New York
You better watch your ass

Eric Garner was tired of being hassled
For selling loosies
"I'm minding my own business officer
I'm minding my business
Just leave me alone."

We all know what happened after that
The cops assaulted him
Pushed his head into the ground
Choked him
Eric Garner died, gasping," I can't breathe."

The other day a car came speeding by me on the freeway
Disappeared into the traffic
A bit later, there they were
A cop writing up a citation
Handing it to the guy
Sitting behind the wheel
And then they both went on their way

Now Eric Garner might not have wanted a citation
For selling loosies
But I'm sure he'd prefer a citation
To what he got

2 Seconds

One one thousand
Two one thousand
Count 'em
Two seconds
It took the cop 2 seconds to shoot Tamir Rice
It took the cop 2 seconds to kill him
He was just a kid
Playing with a toy gun
Oh yeah, Tamir was a black kid

I had a toy gun like that
I'd play on my block
Bang, bang, we'd all blast away
A lot of kids on my block had guns like that
Even Oliver

We'd hide behind cars
Sneak up on each other
Sometimes the cop would walk on by
Never shot at us
Sometimes he'd point his finger at us
"Gotcha!" he'd laugh
We'd go, "bang, bang."
With our toy guns
Even Oliver
Oh yeah, Oliver was a black kid

One one thousand
Two one thousand
Count 'em
Two seconds
I guess Oliver was lucky

Shifting Gears

I know she's no kid
I know she's tired
It's in her voice
Coming through the phone wire
All the way from Colorado

She slides into my ear
At Barack Obama's outpost in Sacramento

"Nice of you to call
But I'm really not interested in voting
I stopped voting years ago."

I expect the "don't bother me" click
But at that moment the door is open
And I step on through

"That's interesting
What made you decide to stop voting?"

"Now Mister, if you're out calling folks
You're just wasting your time
"Cause I'm all done voting"

I think she hears my chuckle
As I say
"Ma'am, I'm a volunteer
Probably about your age
And I've always been interested
In how people decide stuff
And I got plenty of time for you."

Her voice rises
"Hmm, well, when that court gave us Bush
Instead of what's his name
That did it for me."

Suddenly she doesn't seem so tired

"And Clinton, heck,
A little personal integrity would of helped
I mean he was the President."

140

I feel us shifting into first gear
It's as if we're driving on city streets
Heading out, down the Delta

"And that electoral college
I mean this is 2012, not 1776
It makes no sense."

As we shift into second gear
The streets thin out
And the road opens up

I can't hold it back
"You know, you're right on."

"Well, maybe so, maybe not
I'm just trying to get by the best I can.
For me and my daughter."

I decide to take a chance
"How's your daughter doing?"

As we shift into third gear
It's like we're on a two lane black top
With some tight curves
And the river off to the side

She tells me of her 37 year old daughter
With health problems
A minimum wage job
And no health benefits

Politics is now gone
The economy is now gone
We're just people talking about real stuff

As the road dips into a lush green valley
We shift into fourth gear
Passing vineyards and pear orchards

Suddenly she turns to me
"I must admit

Obama's got compassion
He's got compassion
For ordinary, hard working people
I can feel it."
"You can actually feel it?"
She smiles, "Yes, I can."

I glance over
"Well, I do believe we need a lot more compassion."

She laughs
"Me too!"

We drive along in silence
Gradually the city streets reappear
As we pull up to Obama's outpost
I turn to her
"So what do I put down on my paper," I ask

"You can tell them this year
 I'm gonna vote
Tell them this year
 I'm voting for compassion!"

Gerald And Lauree's Deck

"The fool on the hill
Sees the sun going down
And the eyes in his head
See the world spinning round."

I was standing on a hill
Fresh from New York City
So many years ago
Inhaling California
Feeling the world spinning round
Watching the oak trees dance
Deep green against the golden fields
Of Sonoma County

Now, so many years later
On Gerald and Lauree's deck
I still feel the world spinning round
I still watch oak trees dance
Deep green against the golden fields
Of Sonoma County

Our families have driven on many highways
Had our share of motor troubles
Managed to hang in, on some tight curves
Seen some wrecks along the way
And now and then we still
Pull in for a tune up

But today we're on Gerald and Lauree's deck
Feeling the world spinning round
Watching the oak trees dance
Deep green against the golden fields
Of Sonoma county

And from across the table
Gerald laughs and announces
In his deep distinguished court room tone
"Now that you're in your terminal home
Remember, each step is a meditation!"

Freaking Out

I pick up the phone
"Are you sitting down?" you ask
I feel a rumble deep in my gut
"Yes."
"Now don't freak out."

You're good at telling me
Just what you need done
You've been doing that since
Rivkah and I met you and Gerald
Are we talking 40 years now?

"I won't freak out."
But that rumble is squeezing me
Filling my lungs
Blocking my breath

"I've got ALS."

I'm sitting down
I'm not freaking out

I need more air
But the air has all been sucked away

A Piece of Littleton

The day was clear, crisp
The crowd had gathered
The city officials were making speeches
Everyone was looking up at Littleton Alston's sculpture
Remembering that day, September 11, 2001

I stood, watching the arcs of stainless steel rising up
Rising up, from the ground below
The sun touching the holy metal
Bouncing shafts of light into the sky
I stood, watching the metal hands
All trapped in their latticed ball
Entwined, and huddled
In a last embrace
Below the Towers

Littleton, a street kid in Washington, DC
A street kid who knocked on trouble's door
A street kid who walked through that door
And kept right on walking through, to the other side

Littleton, clay, metal, paint, it all breathes when he touches it

I dropped by his studio one day
"How's your 9/11 piece coming?"
"Glad you mentioned it, brother
Now grab those goggles."

Next thing I know, I'm pulling on stainless steel
"Hold it, hold it, now pull, pull on it!"
He's standing on a table above me
Pushing a large round metal piece into the gap my pulling is making

My head is pounding
I'm sure my arms will tear away from my shoulders
"Hold, hold!"
I look up into his face

Eyes leaping from his head
Veins full and throbbing
He has grown to twice his size
And as he pushes the steel down

His sweat drops off onto my face

"Uuuurrrgghhh!"

A wild sound roars from his throat
He has dropped his human self

"Uuuuuurrrrgggghhhh!"

He has become sheer force
His strength feeds me
I pull harder
He pushes harder

"Uuuuuuurrrrgggggghhhhhh!"

And suddenly it's done

His eyes smile
He comes back to earth
"We did it."
And all I can do is exhale and look to see
If my arms are still connected to my shoulders

After the speeches
People keep coming up to Littleton
Honoring him with their feelings
He takes it all in
Returning the honor

After a while Littleton walks over
And embraces us
And I can still feel his sweat on my face

Sacramento Sonata

The Sacramento Bee said
"95 degrees and sunny today."

The guy coming down the block is wearing a coat
Just like the one I left behind
In Omaha, Nebraska
Built for minus zero
Ice and snow

It's hanging below his knees
It weighs close to what he weighs

Well, maybe not if you count
The large, bulging plastic bag
Slung over his shoulder
If you count
The ripped, oversize sneakers
Dragging as he walks
If you count
The crumpled fedora
Riding on his head

He reaches up
With the sleeve of his coat
Wipes his sweaty face

Walking about half a block behind him
Two young ladies who look like they belong
On a COME TO SUNNY CALIFORNIA poster
Are showing it all off

Their swinging shapes
Held firm by
Tight shorts
Tank tops
And flip flops

Across the street
A guy who just got off The Light Rail
Stops and watches
As the California Poster Parade
Struts on by

He lights a cigarette
Blows smoke into the morning air

A joker in a passing car hits his brake
Yells something
The ladies turn, laugh
Yell back
And wave him on

As the California Poster Girls approach
And start to walk around the guy
With the Omaha coat
He turns
Looks at them
Says something

It happens in a second
They stop
One young woman digs in her purse
Reaches over to him
He reaches out
Takes her money
Smiles, shakes his head

The California Girls smile at him
Then walk on by

The guy with the Omaha coat
Turns the corner
And heads down a shady, tree lined street

I reach for my house key
Bringing home
The music of the morning

The Sacramento Bee said
"Tomorrow will be cooler."
But as I think about it
Today is pretty cool
And it's not over yet

Abigail's Breakfast Place

She's deep into her crossword
At the little table facing the sun
The colors of her breakfast scramble catch me
Green onions, red and yellow peppers, and more hidden treasures
Lush coffee smell in the cool San Francisco air
No need to read the menu

"Excuse me," I say
No reply
I try again, then lean over to her table
She looks up, smiles
Points to her lips
Shakes her head, side to side
I nod, shake my head, up and down
Point to her breakfast
Rub my belly, smile back

Her eyes grow brighter
She grins
She takes her pen and writes on her napkin, gives it to me
"It's delicious, Abigail's Special, try it."

Later she looks up, glances over to me, rubs her belly
Her eyes say "How is it?"
My eyes light up
I rub my belly
We both laugh

After a while she gets up to go
She looks over
We nod together
Then she points to the sun
She rubs her belly
I nod, rub my belly and point to the sun
We both smile

As she starts to walk away
She gives me two thumbs up
And we both wave goodbye

It's over too quickly
I was just beginning to learn her language

Just Two Guys

His ass wasn't hanging out
But it could of been
Boxer shorts like a little curtain
Hiding the next act
From the audience

His legs doing all they can
To keep his pants up
That wide forward step
Engineered just right
To keep it all in balance
Occasionally he reaches down
To give those pants a subtle upward tug

He's totally cool
No hesitation, just strong forward motion
His dredlocks swinging to an inner tune

I'm laughing to myself at the comedy act
Walking in front of me
This could be Charlie Chaplin
All over again
But today it's a young black man
Walking in front of me
As I head to Capitol Park
With Poesy, my little, 4 legged
Incarnation of Edgar Allen Poe

A loud crash from behind
Jolts us both
We turn
Expecting to see
Two cars in serious trouble

Nothing
Just a quiet, bright day

"Whoa, that musta been something,"
Comes rolling out of his mouth

"Yeah, whatever happened, I don't want to see it," I laugh

"You and me both."

We're looking over at each other
He shakes his head and announces
 "Crazy ass Sacramento drivers
 What is it with these guys? "

I'm smiling as I catch up to him
"You're right, this place has more crazy ass drivers
Than any place I've lived."

Poesy's wagging her tail
Showing off
She comes over and sniffs his pants leg

"Cute puppy you got there."
He reaches down, scratches her head
She's on her hind legs now
Wanting more
He keeps scratching
We keep talking

Soon we're writing the book
On crazy ass Sacramento drivers
The wonder of little dogs that don't yap
The beauty of having moved here
Him from Philadelphia
Me from what seems like the whole country

He reaches down again
Gives Poesy some more loving
And as we head out he smiles
"Hey, brother, have a nice day."
I smile back
"I will, you too, and watch out for those crazy ass drivers."

I glance over my shoulder
He's disappearing around the corner

He's keeping it all in balance
And so am I

Langston

In 1924 Langston Hughes
Hears America singing

"I, Too, sing America," says Langston
"I am the darker brother
They send me to eat in the kitchen
When company comes…"

As Langston continues reading his poem
I close my eyes
And follow his voice
Down a long path within me

My mother is visiting
We've been invited out
We've been h'ordeuvred and wined
We've been shown the view
And now we're at the table

Dinner is about to start
A door opens
The woman I have not met, enters
She carries a tray
And a large steaming serving dish
Too large

She is older than she looks
Her tired eyes speak
"I'm doing the best I can"

The brown skin of her face
Has been wiped dry
But she missed a spot
A few drops of sweat
Sit just above her eyebrows

Langston leans over, whispers in my ear
"See her, she is the darker sister
To her darker brother
She too eats in the kitchen when company comes
She too hears America singing
And the time is now."

I push my chair back and stand
"Hello, I'm Abe, I don't believe we've met yet."

She looks up at me
A small smile, a nod
"I'm Bernice."
"Hi Bernice, that's heavy, can I help?"
"That's OK, I can manage."
"Oh, I know you can
But you see I'm just a natural born helper."

Her eyes lift up
"Well, I do believe you are."

Later, after dinner, we're leaning
On the counter in the kitchen
Bernice is giving me
Her Grandmother's recipe for
"The best gumbo you'll ever eat."

Langston, steps out from the corner
Bernice and I stop and watch as he
Finishes reading his poem:

"Tomorrow,
I'll sit at the table
When company comes.
Nobody'll dare
Say to me
Eat in the kitchen then.

Besides,
They'll see how beautiful I am
And be ashamed—
I, too, am America."

Catching Up

The three young guys are laughing
Swinging their guitars in the air
The old guy, clutching his violin
Is having trouble catching up

Four mariachis
Coming down my block, late at night
Maybe from some nearby Mexican restaurant

Wide, black sombreros tilting precariously
Black jackets with little silver buckles
Black tight pants with fancy side trim
And bright white boots

Razzle dazzle, flashing in the glint of the street lamps
All heading my way

As the three young guys approach
I pull my dog over
"Buenas noches!"
"Buenas noches!"
"Buenas noches to you."
"Hey amigo, where you get such a little dog?"
"Sacramento SPCA."
"Hey, that's a good place."
Bright eyes
Bright smiles
We laugh as we continue on

The fourth guy
Is still coming, very slowly

As I approach him
I see his white hair
Hanging out under his sombrero
His silver buckles
His fancy side trim
No match for his tired feet
Wobbling in his bright white boots

No laugh
No bright smile
He clutches his violin by the neck
It's hanging real close to the ground
Suddenly he stops
Turns
Walks to a parked car
Leans against it
Catches his breath

I walk over
"You ok?"
"Si."
"You sure?"
"Si, gracias."
He pushes off and continues on

Way down the block
The three young mariachis
Are stuffing their guitars in their car
And waiting for the old man to catch up

I glance back
I know he will never catch up
Unless they slow down

Comrades

His turban is purple
His skin is almost black
His eyes are bright, clear
He is watching the little girl
Jumping in the fountain
In Fremont park

His wife sits close to him
Her hair swept up
With a jeweled pin
Her gold sari in folds around her
She is smiling at the child

There is an empty space
On the bench
Perhaps for one more

I've been unpacking boxes
Hanging up pictures
Shelving books
Gathering another load for Goodwill

And now I've got to pick up Prosecco
For a party at Bob's house

But the kid is playing in the fountain
They are sitting on the bench
The day is sunny, cool and clear
The empty space is calling
Prosecco can wait

Three hours later
He is Jai Singh
She is Indira
I am Ibrahim
And we have journeyed together
To India
To New York
To Seattle
And we are comrades

We have lost our sons
We have shared pain
We have found joy in simple gifts
We have helped people
Create a balance in their lives
We spoken out for civil rights
We have loved
We are loved
We show our pictures

Jai says, "Your daughter
She is beautiful."
"Ah," I say, "Your daughter, she shines
Like your eyes."

As we rise to go
We embrace
Jai smiles
"May God bring us together again."
"That would be wonderful."

I turn and watch them walk away
They hold hands
Just like Rivkah and I

As I walk to my new home
The day is still sunny, cool and clear
And I still need to get that Prosecco!

It's Parkinson's

I'm OK, John says
He reads the message in my eyes
"I love you, man
And I don't want to scrape you off the floor
The banister helps."
I'm OK, John says
So I let it go

Thirty two years of loving his soul
Now Parkinson's has crawled inside
Shuffling his body, messing his mind

Every day he wobbles up
Every day he wobbles down
Two stumbles
Two falls
No blood
No broken bones

In Sonoma we sit in the car
"They're taking pictures of me
That man is watching us."

The wires that go from a battery pack
To his brain help the twitching
But the people he sees
Who are out to get him
Keep showing up

Sue Ellen says
"Sweetheart, that kid is just using his cell phone
That old lady has no weapon in her bag
Those people are not out to get you."
"Yeah," he says
But he goes right on

The day after he pees on the car seat
Because the people across the street
Are spying on him
I bring it up

"It's Parkinson's
It's all Parkinson's."
His eyes tear into me
"But…"
"No buts, it's all Parkinson's."
"But…"
"Don't go with maybe it's the camera
Don't go with maybe it's the people on the corner
Don't go with maybe Sue Ellen is gonna desert you
Don't go there
Just go with 'It's Parkinson's."
My hands on his shoulders
"John, it's Parkinson's, say it!
Say it now!"

His eyes touch mine
My eyes touch his
We start practicing

Three days later we're walking
A crowd of people are standing, talking
John's eyes squint as he stares at them
I watch him twitch
He turns to me
"It's Parkinson's."

Part Two (one year later)

 John and Sue Ellen's holiday card came
A luminous proud peacock
Feathers of iridescent blue, red, green
Rising from the paper are these words:

> *It's Parkinson's* has really helped us both
> Many times over the last year.
> It reminds John
> That his strange thoughts
> Are a result of his disease.

John's eyes still touch mine
My eyes still touch his
We're still practicing

A Short Story

The clerk in Sears knew it all
She answered all my questions
Even asked me some
Laid some options on me I never even knew were there
She looked me right in the eye

She was young, smart, with a sparkle to her style
And she was really tall
She had an open way about her
That invited conversation
I didn't hesitate

She also had a way
Of pulling her shoulders down
In a kind of slouch

As we kept talking
Her slouch reached over
Tapped me on my shoulder
Whispered in my ear
"Go ahead, take a chance, tell her."
I tried to ignore it
"It's not my business."
The tapping wouldn't quit

So I took a chance
"You mind if I tell you a short story?"

She stopped, chuckled
Looked me right in the eye again
"Go for it," she said
And I did

The picture came flying back to me
In sharp detail
Technicolor

Miss Giroux, my high school English teacher
Stopped me in the hallway
As I was heading to my 3rd period class
"Abe, will you come to my office
I want to talk to you."

Miss Giroux was tall
Had red curly hair
Respected us
Showed it
Nobody messed around in her class
We were too busy
Following her through doors of wonder

In her office
Miss Giroux looked me right in the eye
"Abe, don't try to hide your height
Be proud of it
Stand straight
Don't slouch
You're bright
You've got personality."
I missed third period that day
The best period I ever missed

As I finished my story
The young woman leaned in
Reached over
Put her arms around me
"Thank you, thank you so much
I needed to hear that."

She took a deep breath
Pulled her shoulders back
Stood tall in her beauty
We both smiled
We shook hands
"Thank you," I said
I needed to say that."

When I got into my car
I turned to the passenger seat
There was Miss Giroux
Hooking up her seat belt

Poetry With Legs

She walks over from across the bar
Her hips swinging
Rhythm in her stare
Her skirt doing little to hide her long magic legs
Sheathed in black rimmed stockings
And stilettos that cut through the air

"Your beer will have to wait," she says
"I too, am a poet.
I've brought my poetry for you tonight."

She lifts her leg to my table top
Her hands glide up
And linger on her thighs
Slowly, ever so slowly she begins to caress herself

Everything in the place that moves has stopped
Every one sees her poem
It leaps across the floor
Swirling me around, tilting my fantasies
Dusting off long pathways in my mind

And just when I think I will die
She turns to the camera
"Snap it now!" she orders
"I call my poem *Poetry With Legs*."

My Name is Rachel

"My name is Rachel."
Fifty 8th grade students watched her
She slowly pulled up her sleeve
"You ever see this before?"
She pointed to the blue numbers
Stark against her arm
If they were sleepy, they woke up
"Now, you ask me about anything, anything you want."

Slowly the questions came
A quiet stream
She stepped closer
Her hands moving with her words
The current increased
She looked at them all
Calling on them, one by one

Her eyes glistened
Tears came
Still she went on

White caps appeared
The current swelled
More hands went up
She gathered strength
The tears stopped
She was determined
She had stories to tell
The questions grew bolder
She grew stronger

"My little brother, they pulled him
From the barrel he was hiding in."
Eyes wide, total silence
"They shot him, right there."

Much later as the students left the room
They came to her
One by one and embraced her
When the door closed she looked at me
"Nu, was I ok?"
"Yes, Rachel, much more than OK."

At The Library

He sits on a bench
In the shady space, under the tree, near the library
The bags of his life are all around him
His face is streaked with dirt and sweat
He holds a little container of yogurt
He swirls his finger in the yogurt
Pulls some out
Sucks his finger
Smacks his lips
And stares ahead into the sunny space in front of the library

The day camp kids in their bright blue tee shirts
Are laughing and running
In the sunny space in front of the library
Their counselors run with them, waving bright blue banners

Among the day camp back packs
Sits the big red cooler
With lots of little yogurt containers

One kid sits on the grass
He holds a little container of yogurt
He swirls his finger in the yogurt
Pulls some out
Sucks his finger
Smacks his lips
And stares at the man
In the shady space, under the tree, near the library

Listen To The Kids

Funny how one moment in time
Jumps me into another moment in time
So I jump
It's California, 1975

Once again I'm at a conference on juvenile justice
Once again all of us professionals
Deciding what's what, for kids

But I also notice we're all once again
Missing the boat
There are no kids here
There aren't even any wannabe kids here
The conversations are all about OUR ideas

I stand up and ask
"If this is a conference on juvenile justice
How come there are no juveniles here?"
The smack of discomfort hits me in the face
As one by one the professionals cling to their preset agendas
I feel the room shake
As their forgotten youth flounders on the floor

I mumble the serenity prayer
Once again struggling
To accept the things
I cannot change

That day came back to me
As I approached a library here in Sacramento
I knew they had pulled some shelves out
I knew they had removed some books
I know they did it to create a special space
For teens

I didn't plan it
But there they were
Three teens, locking up their bikes
Two more riding up
So I did what I do
I walked over and started a conversation
"What do you guys think of the new teen area?"

"Awesome."
"It's cool."
"No more squeezing in that hallway."
And then the comment that cracks everybody up
"Hey, no more having to smell that stinky bathroom!"
We all laugh and start up the steps

3 kids are sitting at a little table in the teen area
I walk over, same question
"What do you guys think of the new teen area?"
They look up
"It's nice."
"I like it."
"It's cool."
One kid points to the magazine rack
"See, that used to be like the whole teen area."
Another kid says
"Yeah and I'd always get shoved
Every time somebody went to the bathroom."

I borrow some paper
I borrow a pencil
Like I said I didn't plan it
But I was having a good time
I started talking with people

A woman sitting on the floor with her kid
Leans over to me
"They had to take some shelves out.
This is a tight, little library
It gives everybody more space
I think it'll work out fine."

The man in the Giants cap is walking out the door
He's carrying a bunch of books
"I come here a lot. Teenagers need to have a place
I sure did when I was a teenager
What the hell, a little more breathing room won't hurt
You know the old saying
Nothing ventured, nothing gained."

I listen as a man browsing the shelves turns to me

"Too bad they can't just open the upstairs
But I get it
It's a very old building
I'm old, too
A lot of the books they removed
Hadn't been checked out in years
I mean they were real old, like me!"
We laugh together
I put my hand on his shoulder
"Hey, I'm with you!"
We keep laughing

A woman pulling a book off the non- fiction shelf smiles at me
"I love this library.
I go to other libraries too.
If this helps get more kids in, that's just great."

 I keep going up to people
The kids see it
The grown ups see it
And I can feel it

I see another woman, say hello
And then I ask my question
That same question

Instant fury flashes in her eyes
"I don't like it!"
"I'm very angry!"
I listen as her voice rises
And her body stiffens
"This is ruining the library!
Just ruining the library!
Nobody likes it
Just terrible!"
Her rage is roaring out

A man in the corner has turned around
A shocked look on his face
A woman sitting at the table
Turns her head to us
Scrunches up her eyes

I mention that so far all the kids I've talked to
Seem to like it
"Well maybe you should go talk to the adults!" she snarls
The force of her anger feels like a personal slap
Before I can respond
And tell her about the adults I've met
She turns and heads for the front door
I follow, struggling for a conversation
But my words fall on the library floor

As she starts down the steps
She turns, her face contorted in rage
Her last words bounce off the building
"I'm going to take this to the board!"

As I watch her rush off
My mind leaps back to 1975
Back to that conference on juvenile justice
To the adults who know it all
To the adults who have forgotten their youth
To the adults who are prisoners of their preset agendas
They're still here

A Growling Choreography

He squeals
He whines
He growls
His mouth all rusted
Shot to hell

He raises up
On his haunches
Announcing his presence

And then with an awful roar
Gathers up pile after pile
Of tree limbs, leaves
And assorted contraband

Then he heads to his waiting partner
Sitting, rumbling
Open and ready to receive his massive load

The Sacramento Claw
Doing his dance on 13th and Q

Winging It

The crows are here
Black shapes over my downtown home
Crowding out
The early evening winter sky

Swirling
Swooping
The voices of their chorus
Tapping on my windows
Bouncing off roof tops
Sliding off cars

The trees
Stark and skeletal
Beckon to them

They come, settle
Hunker down on all the branches
Their singing now hushed
They sit, they wait
Vibrating

A message rings out
They lift off
And as they again
Fill the sky
I see the school at Bodega Bay
With children running
And Alfred Hitchcock
Filming it all again

2 Bucks, 5 Bucks, 10 Bucks

For Bob Stanley, whose poem "Miracle Shine"
sent my imagination on a journey

Heard about Doc Levin
Goin' out of business?

   No, hell, he been there
   For what? 30 years or so?

Yeah, it's a shame

   Well, he's gettin' up there you know
   A guy's gotta retire sometime

No, It wasn't that
He lost his lease

   No shit. I wonder what he's gonna do
   With all that stuff?

Well, I just walked by there this morning
They're putting everything out for sale
Even hauled over some shopping carts
From the Piggley Wiggley
Filled them up
They got signs all over the place
2 bucks, 5 bucks, 10 bucks
You know, I may just go on back and really check it out

   Hey, I'll go with you
   The fuel pump on my Torino is crapping out
   Sucks up shit from the bottom of the tank
   Stalls now and then
   Maybe I'll get lucky

You still drive that old Torino?

   Yeah, good car
   That baby makes everybody's head turn
   Remember when it was cherry red?

Sure do
WHOA. hey man, this IS your lucky day

How so?

I'll tell you how so
Sitting next to them Piggley Wiggley carts
Are boxes and boxes of Miracle Shine
Never been touched

You gotta be kidding
Professor Frye's Miracle Shine?
God, I remember my dad swore by that stuff
His Dodge was so bright
You'd need a pair of shades just to look at it

C'mon, let's walk over
Before all the good stuff is gone
Could be fuel pump time
For my old Torino
And for sure
She's gonna get
A righteous goin' over
With Miracle Shine
You coming?

You bet
And let's top it off with a nice cold six pack!

The Undead Poets' Society

or

Take Walt Whitman, Henry David Thoreau
And Martin Luther King Jr. On Your Journey

Laughing
  Tumbling
    Be more
    Do more
Give out with a
    "Barbaric Yawp"
And "Suck out all the marrow
      Of Life"

Say it
  Sing it
   Play it
   Pray it
Step out on the road
    And Take It
And when evil tries to soil
    Your precious soul

TURN
  AND FACE IT
   Meet it
    Greet it
     Sing it
      Play it
       Pray it
   And Say It Loud
"Nobody can make you feel
    Like you're nobody."

I Want

I want to meet the guys
Who sat around day after day
And long into those nights
Dreaming up
What Jesus might have said

I want to hang out
With those story tellers
Who sat around their camp fires
Smoking their pipes
Getting higher and higher
As their stories
Got wilder and wilder

I want to join up
With the philosopher kings
And the old Rabbis
Who dictated
All that stuff
About
An eye for an eye
And who can lie down with who
And what evil lurks
In the hearts of men

I want to jump into those
Long conversations
Make sure the guys
Who wrote it all down
Got it just right

But actually
Now that I think about it
I'd rather meet their women

Yeah, while the philosopher kings
And the stoned story tellers
And the holy men
And the guys who
Take dictation
Are putting together their big book

I want to accompany the ladies
Down to the market
Help pick out tonight's dinner
And while the big book
Gets written
The ladies and I
Would be laughing and feasting
And having delicious amorous adventures

And never once
Thinking about
Who can lie down with who
And what evil lurks
In the hearts of men

FANTASTIC FOLKS

I want to thank some fantastic folks who are here with me.

Gerald and Lauree - In our hearts since those crazy days in Sonoma County in 1975, when we all met. We've been up and down and all around and we're "Still Here Now." (Hello, Ram Dass)

Littleton and Anna – Soul mates extraordinaire, and my "brother from another mother."

Gary – My big buddy, builder of high school kids, builder of houses, exuberant life lover.

John and Sue Ellen – Rivkah's best friend from West Coast to East Coast, and our mentor in the Rosebud Puppet theatre, our adventure in storytelling, poetry, puppetry and delighting audiences full of wide-eyed kids, while John's mellowness kept us gently aloft.

Rick and Larry – Here, there and everywhere friends. Everything they do enhances our lives. Their collective art spills out over all they do, and fortunately, they never spill the Bushmills.

Steve – Quintessential wise man – The many roads we travel are strewn with our tall tales, wild projects, family stories, homages to our "brides" and now and then the need to pull over and pee.

Kevin and Lareesa – They loved our dear greyhound, Cleo, and now their two greyhounds pad through their home just like our Cleo did. We were instant friends and compadres and our shared love now includes baby Wyatt. (Not another greyhound!)

Janice – From that day in 1983 when Rivkah announced, "I just met the most amazing woman in the world!" we have shared our lives, our joys, and the depths of our sadness with Janice. Her presence in this world, as a revolutionary, a teacher, an artist, a "bread and butter" friend and as a Dominican sister, is an ongoing example to Rivkah and me of how to change this world for the better, one person at a time.